I0139962

Grace Under Fire

A memoir

Marilyn Leck

Published by Fountain of Life Publisher's House

P. O. Box 922612 Norcross, GA 30010
Phone: 404-936-3989
Please Email Manuscripts to: publish@pariceparker.biz
For all book orders including wholesale email: sales@pariceparker.biz
To request author email: author@pariceparker.biz
www.pariceparker.biz

Fountain of Life Publishing House is committed to excellence in the publishing industry. The Company reflects the philosophy established by the founder, based on Psalm 68:11, *"The Lord gave the word and great was the company of those who published it."*

Book design copyright © 2013 by Parice Parker. All rights reserved.
Cover Design by Parice Parker
Interior design by Phyllis R Brown

Published in the United States of America

ISBN: 978-0-9910627-6-8
12.20.13
Previously published: ISBN: 978-1-61346-253-9

FORWARD

Having been in full-time ministry for over forty years, I have encountered many books about people, their lives, their testimony... but never any so REAl, so MOVING, and so TRANSPARENT in all of my life. You are about to dive into the chapters of this book and once you finish you will never be the same. You will be laughing one minute, sitting on the edge of suspense another minute, then in tears the next minute... but be assured, regardless of the emotion you are experiencing it will pull you into the presence of God as you re-live this testimony of God's mercy, protection, and a woman of God with the ability to forgive, overcome, and breakthrough some of the greatest struggles ever penned in the pages of a book

Pastor Sammy Steven Allen

TABLE OF CONTENTS

Marilyn Leck

INTRODUCTION

I have a story to tell – one that has long been held inside and busting to get out. There is a time and a season to everything that draws breath and this is the season of release what is in me. I hope and pray that by telling my story, it will help all those women and children old enough to read realize they are *not* alone in all their sufferings of abuse by the hands of others and that they will see the hope in my story. So this book is dedicated to all the millions of women and children, and, yes, even men who have endured the violence and fear of abuse and cried the silent tears that no one sees but God himself. This story is as honest as I can make it. So be warned, though it is not specific in nature, I will not hold back. I am telling it from the eyes of a child and then a teen and finally a woman. In the end I will also share what God has done to heal me in all of this.

THE SILENT TEARS

I was born in June – a Father's Day gift of life to my parents – but there was no joy in my birth. My dad wanted a boy, and I came out a girl. My mom and dad were experiencing trouble in their marriage, and they lived with my grandparents.

It is here where my story begins.

I was the first grandchild born into the family on both sides. I was the girl my grandma always wanted, as she had all boys. So when I came home from the hospital, she took charge, letting my mother have little or no say over me.

There was no love lost between mom and grandma. Grandma locked my mom up in a back bedroom and kept her prisoner while my dad was gone. He drove a semi-truck and was gone most of the time. In my grandma's eyes, I became *her* daughter. And that was life.

Mom's family got worried about her and the silence, so they sent the police to the house to check on her, and they found her locked up in the bedroom. They rescued her and sent her back to her family without me. I remained with my grandma. My grandma's children bailed her out of trouble, and they told my dad when he came home that mom had run away to her folks. Never disputing the words of his family, he took custody of me. I would not see my mother, except sporadically, through-out the years of my childhood.

My crib was located in my grandparents' bedroom. With my grandma having diabetes and it taking a turn for the worse, she was confined to a rocking hospital bed in another room. So that left me in the bedroom with my grandpa while dad was gone on the road driving trucks.

It was here where the sexual abuse of my young life began. Grandpa would use me for his own pleasure while I was at a very tender age. I doesn't really matter what he did to me. The fact that he did it started a chain of events in my life that seemed like it would never end. For three years I endured the pain of my grandfather using me as his sexual toy. No one would have believed me, and he told me he would beat me if I told, so I endured. I learned to survive, shut off the tears, and tolerate the pain.

At the age of three, my grandma died in the night. They had the wake in the front room of the house. So for three days and three nights, a dead body resided in our front room. I was forced to sit in that room and look at my grandma's dead body. When people came to view her body, I was always carried up to the casket and made to kiss this dead body. I felt like I was part of a recurring nightmare where everyone wanted to see the grandchild kiss her grandma good-bye. It was awful, and to this day, I'm not too fond of funerals. Nonetheless, I do go and pay my respect to people.

Now my grandpa was alone, and I needed supervision. So I was tossed back and forth between aunts and uncles for about two years. Then they had a family conference and decided that I needed stability. So one of my aunts quit her job and came to live in the home to take care of me. My dad paid her a salary and room and board. But six months into this arrangement, she found a man, got married, and moved out. That once again forced the issue of what do we do with Marilyn.

After another family conference, it was decided that I should have a live-in nanny. And so the interview process started. In the end they decided on a woman who ended up being just as perverted as my grandpa. All of this just set the stage for another round of torture for me. My dad went back on the road, and I was left alone with my grandpa and my nanny.

My grandpa was continuing to abuse me sexually, and soon the nanny got wise, but she had a sick mind also. She started having an affair with my grandpa, and then the two of them decided that they would include me in their games. My grandpa started to share me with this woman.

The things that happened to me have been locked inside the vault of my mind for years now, and the tears that never got shed back then have been released into the Father's loving arms now. This story must be told so you can understand where I have been and why things are as they are in my life now. There are many walking around today, still holding back and shedding silent tears. It is to these people that I speak in this book. You can let it control you, or you can control it. Back then I didn't know how to control it. I only knew how to survive it while I was forced to live it.

Understand that there is real pain in reliving all of this, but there is also healing. For the only way to be healed is to face it all head-on. My childhood was taken from me by circumstances and people. Never once have I ever heard anyone say, "I am sorry." It just was. When that is happening to you and you are in the confines of a house and you don't know what it is like in the outside world, you begin to think this is normal. It wasn't until I as old enough to go to school when I found out what I thought was normal was *not* normal but as sick as it could be. And even then I could not say a word. I learned not how to love, nor was I treated as a family member, so I didn't know how families truly were supposed to be. I learned to survive.

SUFFER THE LITTLE CHILDREN

When a farmer plants a field, he must start at the very beginning. He must cut up or plow the feild before he can plant. This means that he must break the dirt until it's small. These small particles of dirt are spread across the field. So were the years of my life.

Satan was like the farmer. He took control of my life as soon as I exited from my mother's womb. I was born on June 17 to a set of parents who were quarreling. At the age of three months, my parents separated and started divorce proceeding.

My mother took me to the town where her mother lived while my father stayed behind. They were in different states. Like every true divorce situation, there are two sides to every divorce – hers and his. Being only an infant at the time, I must rely on what was told to me. So confusion entered early in my life. Who is telling the truth? Only God knows. And I trust him to guide me through this life. He was always there and near – only I didn't know it until recently.

My mother's side of the story was that she took me with her but I was sick and needed medical attention. She was living with her mom, who was on welfare. The state was going to take her brothers and sisters from their mother. Since she was a minor herself and, of course, I was a minor, the state was going to take her away from my grandma and place me in a foster home. So she called my dad to come and get me. My dad had money, and she did not. She felt I would be better off with him. That's the first rejection of my life entering in so quickly.

My father's side of the story was that he received a letter from my mother saying he should come get me, as she didn't want me. So he got a lawyer and a police officer and came to town to get me. I was literally torn out of my mother's arms and placed with my dad. See how the confusion entered into my life? I had rejection and confusion that would follow and dominate me for many years to come.

When I was one year old, my parents remarried, but this too ended in divorce. I guess former feelings always interfered. The bitterness and strife of the first marriage could not be forgotten or forgiven. I remained with my dad the second time around.

So now I had bitterness, strife, confusion, and rejection in my life. Satan already had a running start. Only one year old and I already had four of Satan's turkeys following me around. In *Joshua 24:17*, it says:

For the Lord our God, he it is that brought us up and out of the land of Egypt, from the house of bondage, and which did these great signs in our sight, and preserved us in all the way wherein we went, and among all the people through whom we passed.

Now this is how my life started, I was born into a house of bondage in the land of Egypt (their sinful world). God promised to deliver me out of that bondage. It is always in *his* timing, never ours. The key words in this passage have *preserved us in all the way wherein we went* and *among the people through whom we passed.*

Each person's life is unique in God's eyes. In his sight you are the one and only. You are precious in *his* eyes.

Thou shall also be a crown of glory in the hand of the Lord, and a royal diadem in the hand of thy God.

Isaiah 62:3

The dictionary says a *diadem* is a crown or tiara. If you check your history books, crowns were only worn by royalty and were usually filled with all the precious jewels of the world – for example: rubies, diamonds, pearls, agates, and almost always they were made of solid gold or silver. If you really study the scripture of Isaiah 62:3, it clearly states that we, as Christians, are more precious to him than all the riches of the earth and that he holds us in *his* hands. That is exciting! No one can ever put me down again, as I'm more precious than all the riches of Earth. And he carries my glory in *his* hand!

Go back to *Joshua 24:17*, where it says: *"and preserved us in all the way wherein we went, and among all the people through whom we passed."* This is a simple biblical truth we sometimes overlook. No matter what the circumstances, the emotions, the people, the intellect, or any given situation, God is there. And he does cover it all with *his* grace. Every life is used of God to *his* Glory, and he'll help us walk through them without getting harmed.

From the age of one to three, I lived with my grandparents. My dad worked, so I saw more of them than my dad. It was during this time of absence that my grandfather started molesting me. The memories of this time are painful to recall, and yet they have helped me minister to many women along the way who were sexually abused as children. Back then it was ignored and swept under the rug. There was no child protection then, and if there was abuse, no one reported anyone.

My grandmother never knew this was going on between me and my grandpa, or if she did, she never let on. She had diabetes and was bedridden, and I can recall lying with her in a hospital bed that rocked back and forth to keep her blood circulating. In my child's mind, I never said a word, as Grandpa said it was a secret we must keep between us. I didn't speak out for fear of being hurt more.

In my third year of life, my grandma passed away. Then it was a matter of having nannies or living with relatives while my dad traveled the roads as a truck driver. I was experiencing my first taste of death with my grandma dying and the casket in the front room. They didn't place them in the funeral homes back then, but they did shortly after her death.

As I said, it was this period of time that I was mourning the death of my grandma and the first time I heard the name of God mentioned or of a placed called heaven. But to this child's mind, heaven was a faraway place. It was certainly not somewhere I wanted to go then.

In *Matthew 11:25-26*, it says: *"At that time Jesus answered and said, 'I thank thee, O Father, Lord of heaven and earth, because thou hast hid these things from the wise and prudent, and has revealed them unto babes. Even, so, Father: for so it seemed good in thy sight.'"*

Also, in *Matthew 18:10,* it says, *"Take heed that ye despise not one of these little ones; for I say unto you, that in heaven their angels do always behold the face of my Father which is in heaven."*

How great to be a child just listening and believing, always seeking and accepting. As adults, we question and explore. We tend to dissect everything that comes our way, while children just accept things that are told them. That's why he says in *Matthew 18:3: "Verily I say unto you, except ye be converted, and become as little children, ye shall **not** enter into the kingdom of heaven."*

Does this mean that we are to all start wearing diapers, drinking bottles, and throwing temper tantrums? No, we're to accept God and *his* son, Jesus Christ, without any questions, for he is truth and truth will set you free.

After my grandma died, I spent the next five years as a traveling piece of furniture. I felt the loss of my grandma acutely through those years. But I kept crying out to God. Mind you, I didn't know God. I only had heard of him but certainly thought it didn't hurt to cry out to him. In my mind's eye, I didn't know who he was; I just knew he was and that he made people die and yet was supposed to make things all right. I don't mean anything bad by this comment, but it's being said with a child's reasoning. Children don't see the world as grownups do. Everything is black or white, good or bad, for them. As adults, we have experience; as children, we only have what we see and feel. They only know as much as you tell them. They ride through on your experiences or their emotions.

This is why God said, *"The sins of the father shall be visited on the sons" (Genesis 20:5)*. If you are living in the world of sin, so shall your children, and if you live on God's grace and perfect will, so shall your children.

In *Matthew 19:14,* it says, *"But Jesus said: 'Suffer little children, and forbid them not, to come unto me: for of such is the kingdom of heaven.'"*

I was like a rubber ball bouncing through different homes and different nannies, and all that happened to me during the rubber bouncing ball years, as I call them; I prayed, as I traveled backward and forward to Jesus for my life. You will see that no matter where you are, he brought me through the very same circumstances and emotions of perhaps where you *are* right now. And what he did for me, he will do for you.

I write this account of my life *not* to glorify the working of the devil and the circumstances I survived but to glorify the Lord of lords and King of kings who delivered me out of the lion's den and kept me from being eaten alive and utterly destroyed and set me free to glorify the God of deliverance. He whom the Lord has set free is free indeed.

I never knew a mom growing up, and in my early years in grade school, they always made us stand up and tell everyone in the class something about ourselves. Everyone would stand up and say something about their mom and dad and brothers and sisters and all about what their family does. When it came to me, I always had to stand up and say I didn't have a mom and my dad drove a truck, so I didn't see him, and all I had was whoever was taking care of me at the time.

MY TRAVELING YEARS

Next came what I call my traveling years. I was more likened to a rubber ball than to a child. I bounced to and fro from one home to another. First, I'd be at a home with my dad, who was Lutheran. Then, I'd stay with an aunt who was an atheist. Next, I would be with another aunt, who was Catholic. After a while housemaids and babysitters were added, but mostly live-in housemaids/nannies were my lot. There was always someone new and never any stability.

I had developed a potluck religion – different views really on whom God was or what he was or if he was! It's confusing for a small child to take in. Everyone was telling me about Jesus and God, but no one could agree on who he was, how he was, or even if he was. All insisted theirs was the only way. As for me, I was in utter confusion, but I wanted to find out who God really was. It was a quest for truth that was to remain with me all of my life.

I remember being so embarrassed having to stand up and say I had no one. And I remember crying in my bed at night, begging this strange something or someone called God to give me a mom to do things with me, love me and tuck me in at night.

The next two years would be turmoil years for my small child's body and mind. I was already being molested by my grandpa, and it was during this time period that I became everyone's sexual toy. My grandpa, my dad, his girlfriends, the nannies – you name it, I was their fair game. I was too young to say anything, and as they all pointed out, who would believe me anyway? I was a child and my dad an upright deacon in the church. They made sure they told everyone that I told tales that weren't true and made things up. So I learned to cooperate, to tolerate, and to be silent. I learned during those times to cry silent tears that no one saw or heard, *not* knowing that God saw and heard my child's tears because he was there all along. "How?" you ask. I didn't die, did I? I lived to tell and to help others along their way. For there are many children and women crying today the silent tears from their hidden hurts of the past are held captive in their minds.

For the next five years, I also spent summer vacations with my mom in her home. It was a free babysitting service in my dad's eyes while he drove truck. He was tired of paying nannies to take care of me. So he would just take me to my mom's and leave me for months on end. I never knew if he would come back. I never told her what was going on. I was too afraid to tell anyone.

The summer I turned eight, my dad and I went to the town where my mom lived to visit her. My dad thought he wanted to remarry her for the third time. But once there he found out she had remarried. Her new husband was nice, and he would sit and play sandcastles with me in the dirt. My dad got jealous because I took to this strange man – my mother's new husband was enjoying just being a child. Jealously rose up in my dad's heart, and he yanked me away from my mom and stomped off with me, and that was the last time I saw her for a while. I would not see my mother again until I was an adult and pregnant with my first set of children.

It was at this point that I deliberately shut off my heart from loving again. The silent tears were there from all the sexual abuse through the years, but the ability of the heart to love was shut up, and I developed a heart of stone. No one would ever hurt me again! That was my vow to myself. Oh, was I wrong on that one, but the tears never flowed on the outside for many, many years to come. I lost the ability to cry, to love, and became a shell of a child. I existed, and that was all.

Shortly after that, I was taken to an aunt and uncle's home while my dad went on vacation. He sent me back a letter saying he was bringing me back a surprise. Two weeks later he returned with a wife and two sisters. What a shock! Here we were a family (according to my dad), bound together by legal papers of matrimony. Yet none of us had ever met the other until two weeks *after* the marriage ceremony. Can you imagine someone walking in and saying to you, "Daughter, here she is? Call her 'Mom'?"

My one uncle later told me that dad couldn't even make up his mind whether to marry her or not. Dad had called him long distance to ask his opinion on the matter. In my child's mind, my dad was insecure. He married for convenience sake and we, the children, would pay the price.

In *Matthew 4:15,* it says, *"And Jesus answering said unto him, 'suffer it to be so now: for thus it becometh us to fulfill all righteousness. Then he suffered him.'"* How did he suffer me? He allowed the suffering in my life. It was through this suffering that I was being molded into what I am today. But during that time, I did *not* understand this at all. I didn't even know God, but looking back, I know he was there. I am alive to speak of it now and to share in hopes that suffering and abused women and children will know that God brought me through and he will bring you through also!

At the time we're going through trials and tribulations, all we can see sometimes is the pain. We walk through them on our emotions, feelings, intellect, and conditional reflexes. By conditioned reflexes, I mean we react a certain way to a given circumstance. A good example of this is: *"If this thing causes me pain, then I must avoid it."* And generally we try to. But we can't. Anytime we walk in the flesh and not the spirit, we fail.

It says in *Ezekiel 39:27-29:*

*When I have brought them again from the people, and gathered them out of their enemies' lands, and am sanctified in them in the sight of many nations; Then shall they know that I **am** the Lord their God, which caused them to be led into captivity among the heathen: but I have gathered them unto their own land, and have left none of them any more there. Neither will I hide my face any more from them: for I have poured out my spirit upon the house of Israel, saith the Lord God.*

It is through our trials and tribulations that God is able to instill faith into our spirits. It is easy to believe when things are sailing along fine, but when things get rough, it's not so easy to believe. It's like sailing a ship across the ocean. Most sailors can do it. But sail a ship across the ocean in the wake of a hurricane – well, that takes an experienced captain. Folks, we need Jesus as our captain or we'll sink. Without him, we are nothing.

In *Romans 5:6,* it says, *"For when we were yet without strength, in due time Christ died for the ungodly."*

That is what I was. There I was, eight years old and full of tribulations and definitely ungodly. I was seeking God but was nowhere near finding him. It was at this point that my life took a sudden turn for the worse. It was here that

Satan took an all-out campaign against me and my life. In *Romans 8:18, "For I reckon that the sufferings of this present time are not worthy to be compared with the glory, which shall be revealed in us."* Praise God! All our tribulations will be turned into God's glory for our lives! Isn't that exciting? The devil tears us down, but God builds us up.

HER HUSBAND'S DAUGHTER

*A*fter my father remarried when I was eight, life quickly settled into a routine of utter disaster. Looking back with an adult's understanding, I can see more clearly now the whys and wherefores of the situations that arose. But living through them back then as a child, I never understood at all. The pain of those years would live with me for many years to come. I already had been sexually abused, lost my ability to cry, and had a stony heart. How much worse could it get?

My father worked nights and slept days. Needless to say, we rarely saw each other. So the major bulk of responsibility of us kids fell on my stepmother, and it certainly was *not* a responsibility she desired or even was prepared to handle.

My stepmother had left her friends, family, and familiar surroundings behind to move here with her new husband. She was not prepared for the acute loneliness she felt. To make matters worse, she didn't feel welcome by her new husband's relatives. Though this was not true, she still felt unwelcome. So she suppressed a deep anger inside that was eventually going to cause havoc and ruin the lives of us kids.

Being the oldest child, she often talked to me of her real feelings and, at the same time, directed the anger toward me. She couldn't lash out at her husband, so she lashed back at me – her husband's daughter. It became an everyday thing for me to hear the following comments: "You're just a package deal. I had to take care of you or your father wouldn't have married me. I really don't want you. I just have to put up with you," or "There must really be something wrong with you. After all, two mothers hate you, and your natural mother didn't want you and neither do I," or "You'll never amount to anything. You're ugly, bad, and unwanted. I wish you were dead."

As you can guess (or maybe you've heard something like this yourself), these comments did not build me up; they just tore me down. They ruined my self-worth and self-respect. About this time she started abusing me in a physical way. At times I had bruises on my body. There were times the bruising was visible that some folks would question me as to how I got them. Well, I lied and would continue to lie until my stepmother couldn't beat me anymore. They knew I'd lied by the nature of the bruises. But honestly, what kid wants to tell others their parents beat them?

An abused child generally will not snitch on a parent either out of fear of another beating or a warped sense of familiarity. By this, I mean the beatings are associated by love or with love. So therefore, in the child's mind and reasoning power, you're not loved unless you are being beaten on. In actuality, just the opposite is true.

It is here that one of God's principles was broken. In *Matthew 18:6,* it says, *"But whoso shall offend one of these little ones which believe in me, it were better for him that a millstone were hanged about his neck and that he were drowned in the depth of the sea."*

Also, in *Matthew 18:10,* it says, *"Take heed that ye despise not one of these little ones for I say unto you, that in heaven their angels do always behold the face of my Father which is in heaven."*

In our household, all the children were divided by discord and trauma. We were so traumatized by circumstances that we literally never learned to be a family. We never even learned to be brothers and sisters. We were just learning to exist in a world devoid of all feelings. In *Mark 3:25,* it says, *"And if a house be divided against itself, that house cannot stand."*

Our household was never meant to stand. Our family was torn up by all the strife and confusion. I learned very quickly that emotions were not an acceptable item. I learned to have a hard heart. In my case, it just got harder and colder. I would endure pain and suffering in silence. In no way would I ever give them the satisfaction of seeing me hurt or cry. My self-esteem and self-respect were totally lost.

In *James 1:8,* it says, *"A double minded man is unstable in all his ways."* Well, my stepmom was unstable. We never knew what was going to happen next or in which direction she would go. When other people were around, she was nice, polite, and innocent. But when we were alone with her, there was violence.

And in *Ephesians 6:4,* it says, *"And ye fathers provoke not your children to wrath: but bring them up in the nurture and admonition of the Lord."* This passage is the second half of *Ephesians 6:1,* which says, *"Children, obey your parents in the lord: for this is right."* The key words are: *obey your parents in the Lord.*

You see, parents, if we're not walking with God in our daily lives and setting the proper examples for our children, then we can't expect our children to be obedient and respectful. We, as parents, set the examples for their lives. Children look at us and think, *if it's all right for mom and dad, it's all right for me.* Wrong! Children grow into adults by copying after those things in their lives that surround them. Parents, teachers, friends, and neighbors *all* have input into a child's life.

God says, *"Provoke not your children to wrath"* *(Ephesians 6:4).* Do you know why? Because when you make your children angry, you open the doors for sin and Satan to enter in. What sins? So glad you asked! Wrath brings in rebellion, bitterness, anger, strife, jealousy, and un-forgiveness, just to name a few. Also, it can cause your children to be discouraged. *Colossians 3:14 says, "And above all these things put on charity, which is the bond of perfectness."*

Charity means love. In order to get love, you have to give love, and the only way to give love is to know love, and the only way to know love is to know God. For God is love! Once you know God, you know Jesus. Once you know Jesus, you know hope. Jesus is the hope of your heart. The hope of the heart is the hope of the home. And the hope of the home is the hope of the world. As you can see, this is a chain reaction snowball that grows as it goes. And as you can see by my own childhood, a home without Jesus is barren of all good things.

Parents, why do you think there's so many problems in the homes these days? In *Colossians 3:2*, it says, *"Set your affection on things above, not on things on the earth."* When God isn't present, then the devil is, pure and simple. In *Ephesians 6:12,* it says, *"For we wrestle not against flesh and blood, but against principalities, against powders, against the rulers of the darkness of this world, against spiritual wickedness in high places."*

It's not the person doing those things that hurt you but the spirit that operates through them. Satan has many spirits that come from the pits of darkness that come against us on assignments of destruction. The only way to drive victory over them is through the blood of Jesus Christ. Because he fought all our battles for us while he hung on the cross, we have victory in and through him.

It's normal for children to want to copy after adults. That's why little girls love to play house and copy our mannerisms. It is the same with little boys. They copy their father's mannerisms. We, as adults, have to decide: are we going to copy Christ or the devil? We cannot serve two masters. We will love the one and hate the other. Which one do you serve? That is something only you can answer.

ARE YOU MY MOM?

When I was six, my dad decided that he would take cross-country runs, and that put him on the road almost all the time. He was seldom at home. In some respects I didn't know I had a dad because he was never there. And yet in my child's heart, I love my dad.

When I was seven, dad came home more on weekends. That sounds like it would be great, but my own dad joined the crowd, and he too used me sexually. It was like living in a nightmare all the time, but by that time, I was numb to it all. I was like the mice in science that eat only when the light comes on or the bell rings. Whenever one of them said they needed me, I just lay on the bed and waited. One way or the other, they would have their way with me. Sometimes, it was one, sometimes two, and at other times all three of them. I continued to cry silent tears and held on to my survival.

This went on until I was eight years old. Then dad left on a road trip. After being gone for two weeks, he returned home with a surprise for me. He had gotten married to a bartender and brought her and her two girls (my new stepsisters) home with him. All he said was, "This is your new mom."

I never laid eyes on her or her on me. And it was instant dislike! I felt funny inside and asked dad, "What do I call her?" He said, "You call her mom." So I did when he was around, but when he was gone, I was told to never call her that unless he was around or we were in public. And she told me never to call her two daughters "sister," as they weren't my sisters and they never would be my sisters.

Dad quit his truck-driving job and took a job in a local plant making tractors and tractor parts. He worked nights and slept days. We went to school days and sleep nights. So basically, I didn't see much of dad for quite a few years. This left me at the mercy of my stepmom and my grandpa. All this time, my grandpa continued his use of my body but learned to be sneakier about it. I hated life, but I learned to escape into a make-believe world where I would go and lose reality, becoming whatever character I was reading in whatever book I had. I loved to read, as it took me off in imagination to a place where I didn't have to deal with the realities of life. I loved childhood books like *Snow White and The Seven Dwarfs, Hansel and Gretel, Rumpelstiltskin* – all the stories that had mean stepmoms so I could hate them as I did my own stepmom. There was one truth back then: there was no love lost between her and me. She tormented me to no end, and I resented and hated her all the way.

My stepmom told me several times that I was not wanted, that I was a package deal, and that she had to put up with me in order to be with my dad and have him raise her two girls.

I felt so alone – more silent tears. By then, I would not dream of giving anyone the satisfaction of seeing me cry. And it still bothers me today to cry in public or have anyone see me cry. But God has given me the ability to shed tears once again, only this time not in pain but in compassion for others.

One of the things my stepmom would do was stand me in front of a mirror and make me say, "I am ugly," and "no one wants me," and "I don't deserve to live." The truth of the matter was I really didn't want to live. I thought there was no reason to live.

It seemed to be one of her favorite taunts to tell me, "Your mom gave you away, and I don't want you. So that makes two moms who don't want you. Just get used to it! If two moms don't want you, there is something wrong with you, and no one will ever want you."

That stuck in my spirit for a long time. Be careful what you say to your children because it does get deep down inside of them. If told something over and over again, they will start to believe it as gospel truth, even if it is a bold-faced lie!

Summer was over, and my dad changed to second shift so that he could be home more and spend time with us. But his time with me was always in the dead of night. Usually grandpa would have his way and then dad. It was a nightmare for me. In all of that, I learned more about survival. I existed but did not *live*.

I started school along with my sisters (as the world saw them), but to me I had to live in denial. The oldest "new" sister was one year younger than I. She went to the same school as I did. When people asked if I was her sister, she always told them no, and I would not answer anyone. I just went my own way. I had learned to live in silence, and few got close to me in school. They did not – could not – understand the hard life I had at home or the millions of unshed tears inside of me.

A LOVING FAMILY ... NOT!

I still remember the day my dad brought his "new family" home. It was a complete shock to me when he introduced this strange woman and her two little girls. He too just casually said, "This is your new mom and sisters." And then he walked away. Even if he was just in the other room talking to my grandpa and uncle who lived with us, he wasn't with me. What was I supposed to do with this woman? I didn't know her at all and had never met her! And now he tells me to be happy for this is my new mom. Give me a break!

All I could relate to was the nanny and what she had been doing to me and my grandpa. What was I supposed to feel inside but raving fear? My dad just stated so matter-of-factly, as if everyone just springs a strange woman and two kids on their child and says, "Oh, by the way, this is your mom and two sisters." Gee, isn't that like cruel beans?

So I walked in and asked shyly, "Are you my mom." She just stared at me and said, "Well, I guess so," and didn't talk to me for a long time. I was a child and thought, *wow!*

Kids to play with. But they would not play with me. They clung to their mother and rightfully so. I didn't know it then, but they were just as shocked as I was. They didn't know what to think or anything, but this was their real mom. Me? I was with a stranger? Obviously, she did not like me. The only time she spoke or smiled at me was when my dad would enter the room.

For a while, it was like Christmas. Dad went shopping, and her girls got all new clothes while I just got what I had. I guess they had come with just the clothes on their backs. Then it was time for Dad to go to work in the factory. He no longer would drive truck but would work third shift from then on. "mom" set to putting us kids in school. The youngest was not in school yet.

I was still in the parochial school, so the oldest sister had to go there also. The school had a choir that sang on Sunday in the church service and on holidays (especially Christmas) sang in concert for the church. The oldest sister decided to sing in the choir. I wanted to also. She got picked and I didn't. I was disappointed. Then they had tryouts again, and I was picked on the second tryout. I remember coming home so excited because I was going to sing in the choir. But my stepmom just had to bust my bubble. She told me the only reason I got on the choir with her daughter was because she called and talked to the principal and paid him to put me on the choir. I cried all night long, and the next day I quit the choir. There was no joy in it for me. I believed her. She was so convincing. I was angry, hurt, and humiliated. So my sister got to sing and I didn't. Because of that, I have not liked to sing in front of anyone since.

When school was out that first year, we were what my dad called a loving family – not! No way!

I had always had a birthday party, and my dad never said to not have one. I suppose I should have been smart enough to ask, but I really did not think that anything would be different. Dad always had me just invite neighborhood kids over for a birthday cake and ice cream. So I did just that, only to have them show up for it and my stepmom embarrass me by saying there was no birthday party. She said I had told them all a lie and they could not come in. She spanked me good with a belt and told me never to do it again. Of course, when her girls' birthday rolled around, they got parties. My heart broke. I never asked anybody over to my home again. I made no attempt to make friends ever again until years later when God got a hold of me.

My stepmom was nice to me when Dad was around but never when he was gone. If she got mad at me, she would grab me by the hair and slam my head on the wooden windowsills. It hurt, gave me headaches, and would cause problems for me for years to come. I would have temporary blackouts, later to find out they were petit mal seizures that lasted only a few seconds. I never had to be on medicine for them. I just knew when they happened. After a year of this, dad came home early one night and caught her slamming my head on the windowsill, and he grabbed her by her hair and slammed her head into the wall of the kitchen. He told her never to let him catch her doing that to me again. She said she wouldn't, but she only did other things then, like stabbing me with a pair of scissors or with a knife. I carry those scars on my body today. God saw fit in all of this to protect me from death itself.

By the end of fifth grade, dad and stepmom were fighting like cats and dogs. My grandpa was making passes at my stepmom when dad was gone. She complained, only to have him believe my grandpa and not her. She got angry and tried to push grandpa down the stairs to kill him but that didn't work. So she decided to take her two girls and go to her friend's farm and divorce my dad.

She decided that she would not leave me behind. When dad got home from work in the morning, he would come and take me home, as she didn't want me anyhow. There I was, a little child caught between the devil and his imps – my grandpa who was molesting me and this woman who hated me and would send me back in the morning with my dad. I didn't get to make a choice, as she made it for me and dragged me off screaming.

I spent the night in the strange people's house. I didn't know them from Adam. I was in a tough spot with these two kids who were supposed to be my sisters – but I couldn't call them that – and a woman who hated my guts. All I could do was wonder if dad would come and get me or not.

One morning my stepmom woke me up, told me to gather what clothes I had with me, and told me to be ready, for my dad was on the way to get me. I was sitting on the porch with my bag of clothes, waiting for my dad, when he drove up. And drive up, he did. Only he by passed me and went in to talk to her. When he came out, I walked with him to the car with my bag of clothes, fully expecting to go home with him. He hugged me, got in his car, and left me standing in the driveway, watching him drive out of my life.

I was crying (more like sobbing) by then. Why did my dad leave me? Why hadn't he taken me with him? I was standing there, watching dad drive away, thinking I had lost him forever, and my stepmom was yelling my name to come into the house immediately. It wasn't in a nice way she was asking me to do so. I felt so alone and so forsaken. I have always had this fear of abandonment deep inside of me and a fear of being alone. It would haunt me for years to come.

What was I going to do now? I stood in the driveway, watching until I couldn't see the car anymore. To this day that picture and those emotions I felt at the time are burnt into my memory bank. God has taken the pain from that picture, but he has me remember it so I can relate to others who feel so alone and deserted. For at that moment in time, my heart broke, and it was at that point that I became numb and my tears stopped. I vowed I would never hurt like that again!

It was three days before I saw my Father again. He finally came. When he did, I expected him to take just me home, but he took all of us home, only it was to a new home. I say the word *home* loosely, as we never ever had a home, only a building called a house. There never was laughter or love in that place, only hatred and a life of pretending. What the world saw was a perfect family, but what we all saw was hell on earth fueled by hatred and bitterness.

It lasted for a short season. Finally, my stepmom filed the divorce papers, only to find out she was pregnant with my half-sister. So they stayed together and canceled the divorce for the sake of the baby. But nothing changed, and the abuse went on. My grandpa was out of the picture because dad had my aunt and uncle move in to take care of him while he moved his family into the new home. Shortly thereafter, my grandpa was placed in a crazy ward in some hospital far away from where we lived.

The things dad did never stopped. He continued to molest me, and he began molesting my youngest stepsister to the point she became pregnant with his child. He and my stepmom locked her up in a bedroom and told all the neighbors and everyone they knew that she was in some other state living with relatives there. The only time she was allowed out of her bedroom was when she had to go to the bathroom or eat or go to the doctor. How they got her to the doctor without neighbors seeing her, I will never know. My suspicion was that they took her out the garage door and had her lay down in the back seat until they were out of the neighborhood and could not be seen by neighbors.

My dad and stepmom paid the doctor under the table to put their names as the baby's parents on the birth certificate, and then they adopted the baby out. She went through her own hell. All of them did, and each probably has their own story inside of them, but I can only speak for my side of the story, not theirs.

Later, when she supposedly came back home from living elsewhere, my so-called parents told everyone that she wasn't quite right in the head, as she had been raped and lost her baby, and that no one should believe anything she had to say. Everyone believed my so-called parents.

My oldest stepsister and I went to the same junior high school after we were settled down into our new home. It was a few blocks from our home, and we walked to school. She walked by herself, and I walked by myself. After all, our last names were different, and she would never say I was her sister because her mom drilled in all our heads that we were not sisters and could not say we were. So that was the rule we lived by.

While in this school, I had to take gym, and it was my first experience of having to wear a gym suit – you know, the one-piece shorts and top kind – which leads me to my next story.

One day, my sister painted the bathroom with toothpaste and left it. When my stepmom asked who did it, they both said I did. Of course I denied it because I did not do it. But she said I was a liar, and she beat me with a leather belt that had a three-dimensional bronze belt buckle of a bronco rider on his bucking bronco. It was thicker than the belt and solid brass. It was this belt buckle that was at the whipping end of the belt on me. It left cuts and bruises all over my back and arms and legs. I squirmed, and it made her madder, so she kept on hitting me.

I lay in bed that night crying, and it was the first time I reached out to God. I didn't know God, only that there was a God. So I remember saying, "God, I don't know if you are real or not, and I don't even know if there is a placed called heaven. I hear them talk about it, but no one seems to know much about it around here. But God, if this is all the life I have and there really is a placed called heaven and you really are God, will you please come and take me there? I don't want to stay here anymore. I don't want to live this way. It hurts, God. Please take me home right now. I want to die, God. Please take me home."

Well, God heard my plea. I don't know if it was Jesus or an angel, but I know there was a figure of a man surrounded by bright light at the end of my bed. And he never moved his mouth once, but I understood every word he said to me. He said, "Mariyln, you don't understand now, but you will one day. I can't take you now. It is not your time. And one day you will know love and you will find the mother you seek and she will love you. Be patient and know I will protect you, and when you get older, you will understand."

I felt peace, but I was still bruised, hurt, and bleeding. The next morning I got up, sore and bruised. The bleeding had stopped. My so-called mom dressed me in jeans and a long-sleeved shirt and sent me off to school. Needless to say, whenever someone touched me, I'd draw back, and I would hurt from the bruising. Well, it happened to be gym day that day. I told the teacher I didn't feel well and didn't want to participate. She said I still had to wear my gym outfit. I told her I didn't want to. She said I had to, and after a few minutes of arguing, she ordered me into the bathroom to change into my outfit. So I ran into the bathroom and locked myself in.

When I didn't come out when the teacher expected, she came in to get me, but I was still locked inside the bathroom stall. She told me to quit playing games and come out. I told her I didn't want to. She ordered me to get out of there, and that's when she saw all the bruises. She asked me what had happened. I told her I ran into a door at home after tripping. I hung my head; I couldn't look her in the eye. I was scared to tell the truth on how they got there. But she knew I didn't run into the door. She knelt down and hugged me with tears in her eyes. She said, "Honey, follow me," and she took me to the school nurse.

They didn't have any child protection laws, but they called my parents to come to the school. My dad was angry when he saw the bruises on me, and yet he did nothing but yell at my stepmom when I got home. The school told them both that if they ever saw me at school with bruises like that again, they would call the law on them. Everyone went back to routine on the home front, but whenever she beat me, I had to stay home until the bruising was gone. She just told them I had the flu or whatever suited her fancy at the time. So the school never saw any more bruising. I was just labeled a sickly child by them all.

By the end of the school year, my tears were gone. My heart became hard, and I made a vow that no one would hurt me again and I would never see anyone hurt as I hurt inside again. I had resigned myself to the fact that my life would be anything but normal according the kids in school, and I would never have any reports of fun times with my family like them.

WATCHING MY EVERY MOVE

We were children, and we wanted to play like all other children. At times, we would be allowed to go outside and play with the neighborhood kids. We grew up with lots of children around us, but few were allowed to play with us, especially with me. My stepmom was paranoid about what I would say to others and if they would believe her or me. So whenever she saw me having fun with the other kids, she would call me and tell me I had to stay in. She would tell the others and me that if I stayed outside for any length of time, I would have sunstroke. She had a lot of the neighbors believing I had a bad heart because she would make me come in, and if she didn't make me come in, she would make me sit down on the stoop of the front porch and watch the other kids play, saying I would have a sunstroke if I got too active. This, of course, was a lie, but whoever questioned her? She was an adult, and I was but a child who just remained silent.

I entered the high school years as a sophomore and started in the school. It was clear across town and far away from them all. My oldest stepsister was still in junior high school. So I was given one year of pure bliss alone and away from the rest of them. My stepsister wasn't there to come home and tell my stepmom everything I did at school. I felt like I had been given a pass to heaven. I managed to make a few friends there. The gym teacher in high school recognized that I was a teenager that needed help and was hurting. So she befriended me and reached out to me. I was to find out she was a Christian and would tell me about Jesus, how he loved the little children and that when I couldn't talk to anyone else, I could always talk to him. It seemed that God was giving me little reassurances along the way of my childhood torment. To this day, I love that woman and respect her a lot. As a young teen, I didn't understand all things, but one thing I did understand was that some guy named Jesus who died long ago could hear me if I talked to him. And when things got where I couldn't handle them, I would just pretend he was there and talk to him about the things in my heart.

There were times when she would want to do something with me special. She would ask my stepmom on the phone if she could take me home with her after school and help her do some stuff around her house that she couldn't do. Of course, since it was a teacher asking, my stepmom was afraid to say no, so she gave permission for me to come over for a couple of hours. We would go to her house, and she would fix us some supper, and we wouldn't do anything but sit and talk. She even made me laugh a little. It felt so good to know that someone actually wanted to be around me. I didn't understand how a stranger could like me but my so-called mom and family could not. At least I got a year of this good treatment.

However, it came to a screeching halt the next year, as my stepsister joined the ranks of the school alumni. It also put an end to what I could do and not do, as everything that I did was reported back home. The visits to the teacher ended, as she retired the year that my sister came to the school and we got a new gym teacher.

I don't know how to put it tactfully, but I was a teenager, and in those years, certain things of puberty start appearing. One was hair on our legs, and the other was our monthly cycles. When it came to the hair on our legs, my stepsister was allowed to shave her legs and be normal. But my stepmom would *not* allow me to shave. Well, I grew black hair on a fair skin, and it stuck out and was thick.

It seemed like such a little thing, but I was made fun of by the other kids all the time. They would make such cruel remarks as "Don't tumble over the bushes when you walk by" or "Look out! Here comes the forest tree." They would say these things out loud so the whole class could hear it, and the rest of the class would giggle and point at me and my legs. I hated it, was embarrassed, and cried inside. One of the classes that this happened in the most was Spanish class. I never understood why the teacher would not stop them from doing it, as she laughed right along with the kids.

It got to be so bad. I was tormented already at home. I couldn't stand all of this, so I would tell the teacher I had to go to the nurse's station and take a pill. She would dismiss me from class. Once in the hallway, I would make my way to the bathroom and hide out in there until the bell rang. I never did make it back to class. When the teacher would ask me why I never same back to class after taking the pill, I told her I fell asleep after I took it. She seemed to accept that explanation until one day she ate lunch in the teacher's lounge and there sat the school nurse. She asked the nurse what was wrong with me because I never came back from taking the pill. It was then that she found out I had lied all along. That made it worse for me. Never tell a lie. It is always exposed. I got called into the school office and was raked over the coals for ditching class and lying to the nurse and to the teacher. Then they called my home to tell my parents. My stepmom got the call. I admit I needed punishment but not a beating. We never got spanked; we got beat. Needless to say, I never pulled that one again. I just suffered the torment in silence.

My stepmom was dressed in the styles that were back then. I was not permitted to dress in the latest styles. One day my stepmom made me wear a dress that was in style in the 1920's – the ones with long padded shoulders that made you look like an army colonel. I cried. It was the first time in a long time that she saw me cry, and I remember her smirking as she sent me off to school. I didn't have a choice but to walk into the school dressed like a freak! And the kids made sure I really knew how awful I looked. I was tormented all day. When I got home, I changed into play clothes. I asked if I could ride my bike, and for once she said I could. I took those clothes out the back door, got on my bike, rode around the block, and threw them in someone else's garbage can. I never wore that dress again, and she could never find it again. That was the only time I rebelled against her.

In high school, there were dances and parties, and my sister got to go, while I couldn't. No one would ask me anyhow because I had become the freak at school and the brunt of everyone's jokes.

My stepsister started sneaking around to see this boy at school, and at one point, she thought she was pregnant by him. Everyone knew this but my stepmom. Somehow the rumor got back to her that one of her girls was pregnant, and she immediately assumed it was me, as her girls would never do anything like that. Frankly, I was surprised. It wasn't because of the things my dad was doing to me. I was the one who got a beating over it and taken to the doctor, only for her to be told I wasn't pregnant. It didn't stop there. From that day on, every time she knew I was menstruating, she would undo the used pads and inspect every single one of them in the garbage can before she threw them away. If there wasn't enough blood on the pad to her satisfaction, she would say I was messing around, and she would beat me with that infamous belt.

As I got older, it was harder to beat me. She had to catch me first, but if I ran, she would become angrier, and she would grab the nearest thing to punish me with. In most cases it was a knife or a pair of scissors. To this day I carry the scars on my arms and parts of my body where she would stab me with these objects, not enough to bleed bad but enough to inflict pain and leave small scars. I hated my life. I hated my home, and I hated my stepmom and sisters with a passion. And I had started to hate my dad not only for doing the things he did to me but also for looking the other way when things happened.

When my dad and stepmom got in horrible fights, they would call us out of the bedrooms, and we would have to choose sides. It didn't matter which side you chose because the other would beat you for not taking their side when all was said and done. It was a no-win issue. So we just remained silent.

My stepmom moved her mom into the home. Her mom was elderly, and my stepmom took grandma's Social Security check every month. I loved my grandma! She was nice to me, but she was frail and couldn't protect me. She would sneak in a hug once in a while and tell me that her daughter had always been crazy and she was sorry that I was being treated so badly. No one would listen to her either, and eventually she was placed in a nursing home, where she died.

I remember hearing my stepmom go into the bedroom and hearing the thumps where she would be hitting my baby half-sister and the baby would be screaming. I knew she was hitting her, but I couldn't say a word. When dad came home and saw the bruises on the baby, he would ask her what happened, and she would say she rolled off the bed or she fell. It was always something but never the truth. I don't think she could tell the truth.

There were times I remember when my stepmom would pull up a kitchen chair and watch the clothes tumble on the side window dryer. We would actually hear her carrying on conversations with the clothes in the dryer and laugh and clap her hands. She would do this often. Every time she did the laundry, she had these conversations with the clothes in the dryer. When the clothes were done, she would come out and she would beat me, and she started beating some of her other children but never her oldest. We knew that when the clothes were done, one of us would get a beating. For the most part, it was me. I didn't like the beatings, but often during these times, I would get between her and the others and take their place. I knew the pain, and I didn't want to see them go through it, so I would aggravate her and make her chase me. When she caught me, she would either beat me with the belt or stab me with the scissors.

I would never say a word. My stepmom did no housework. We did it all. Saturday was ironing day. She divided the ironing up in half. My oldest stepsister had to do half, and I had to do half. When it was done, she would do inspection to make sure we had done it right. Of course, the stepsister's was always perfect, but she always found something wrong in mine, whether there was or not. She would go into a rage and grab everything off the hangers that I did, wad them up and wrinkle them back up, throw them on the bed, and make me re-iron them. All my Saturdays consisted of was ironing and redoing ironing while my other sisters got to play outside and have fun. And each time she wadded the clothes up, I would get beaten with the belt. That was life in my home.

When it came to mealtime, the food was set out on the table. I was always placed across the table from her. She would fill my plate up with food in such large proportions that I could not eat it all. We were not allowed to leave the table until it was all eaten. But we didn't just eat the food; we ate it in a specific order. We ate our meat, then our potatoes, and then our vegetables. We didn't drink anything unless she let us. It seems like a weird comment to say, "Until she let us." It is how she controlled how we ate. If I didn't eat it fast enough or if I tried to eat anything else until the meat was completely gone, I would get kicked under the able hard in the shins. Once the meat was gone, we were allowed to drink two swallows of the drink on the table. My shins were always bruised. One day she made a mistake and kicked my dad instead of me, as his legs were stuck out under the table. He asked her why she kicked him, and she told him her leg had a twitch in it. When she got a chance, she kicked me harder and gave one of those looks to say, "Don't say a word or you are mine." She didn't have to worry; I wasn't going to say a word.

One thing I leaned well in my childhood years was that I couldn't trust adults. I knew the neighbors heard our screams, but none of them ever said a word. They all looked the other way, not wanting to get involved. So the abuse went on. I learned to cry in silence, not to show emotion, and, above all else, I learned what not to be when I grew up. I vowed that should I ever grow up and have kids, I would never treat them as animals, nor would I ever cause anyone the pain that I had endured. Something else happened in those childhood years. I learned a conditioned reflex that would become an unconscious thing with me for years to come. I learned that if someone says they love you, they beat you. "If you didn't beat me, you didn't love me." Just like the lab mice who don't eat unless the bell dings, I knew you didn't love me, if you didn't beat me. Of course this was a lie, but I didn't know it at the time. That unconscious mode of thinking had been planted deep within me.

My two years in junior high passed quickly. The only memories I had of that time were all hurtful, and I became even more reclusive, preferring to stay to myself rather than mix with others. My stepmom had planted a seed inside of me that I was ugly, unwanted, and certainly unlovable. So I became defeated with the mind-set of "why bother?" No one wanted to be around me anyhow. My stepsister proved that to me every time someone would ask if she was my sister and she would say no way, even that she never saw me before in her life. She too joined in the tormenting comments of the others. I guess for her, it was a way to be part of the "in crowd" and be accepted by her peers. I just stayed away from her and the others.

Next would be my senior high years, and gratefully I got one year there without my sister being around to spy on me. I did manage to make a few friends there, not many, but a few. I was still too cautious for my own good. I was never allowed to bring my friends home, as that was forbidden. The high school years passed quickly, and my best friend lived not far from me. She was an outcast also. Her name was Susan, but I called her Sue. Well, Sue and I decided that we would join the navy, see the world, and never come home again. That way we would both be safe. She had a bad childhood also. To make a long story short, she went into the navy, and I was turned down – not because I didn't pass the entrance tests, but because I was born blind in one eye. I couldn't pass their eye exam requirements. So I took office skills as my major the last two years of high school.

During my high school years, my so-called parents continued to fight, and it was never peaceful in our home. All we ever heard was them yelling and screaming at each other. Whenever my stepmom got mad at my dad, she would take her oldest daughter and go shopping and spend all kinds of money on his credit cards and give her stuff, while I did without, as did the younger sisters. She didn't really care, as her youngest daughter was about to enter kindergarten, and she gloated and bragged how she was going to leave my dad and me when the youngest entered kindergarten. That never happened, as she became pregnant once again. I graduated in June at age fifteen (I wasn't quite sixteen), and in November, my brother was born. Because he was the boy my dad always wanted, she had leverage over him now. She used it to the hilt, and my dad agreed to stay with her and finish raising all the children.

My time at home was always in my bedroom. The only times I really came out was to eat, potty, or clean up around the home. And if company came to visit her and dad, I had to stay in my room and could not come out until they left. They came to see them, not us.

MOVING OUT

I was still living at home after graduation but was working full time doing office work. After my brother was born, my oldest stepsister held and fed the baby, but if I went near him or tried to hold him, my stepmom would get in my face and scream, "That's my baby and *not* yours, so you stay away from my baby! I don't want you touching him ever!"

Oh, but I couldn't stand what she was doing to him. If he got a dirty diaper, she would take the soil out of the diaper and scrub his face in it, often shoving it up his nose and into his mouth. I tried to protect him; I would scream at her to stop. She would backhand me, and soon I gave up. My brother survived all of that.

I was afraid to move out because I was scared my stepmother would hurt the others if I wasn't there to make sure she didn't harm them. We kids used to sleep in shifts at night just to make sure she didn't come in and harm any of us as we slept. The only one who had nothing to worry about was the oldest stepdaughter, as she had favor with my stepmom (perhaps because she looked like her). To the rest of us, she showed no favor. Sometimes I would lie and say I did things just so she would beat me and *not* them. I remember telling the neighbors how she had such a brat of a daughter and how I was uncontrollable.

Life was anything but cool. The day came when I got brave enough to move out and share an apartment with two other girls from work. That was a good move on my part, and I felt my youngest stepsister was big enough and so were my half-sister and half-brother that they could take care of themselves. How wrong I was, but at least I was out of there.

Well, I found myself in a whole new world. I wasn't prepared for life outside my parents. I was never taught to handle money, and I learned the hard way and finally figured out that bills had to be paid first. I went into a civil service job and worked as a civilian on a military base. In the meantime, my older stepsister married a classmate of mine from high school. Her mother-in-law had grandchildren by a stepdaughter who separated from her husband. Her son had the girls – a set of twins, ages six and one age five. The grandmother approached me and asked if I would babysit the kids at night while the dad worked. I agreed, so now I was working days and babysitting the girls at night.

Well, he showed me some kindness, and for all the wrong reasons, I married him after a year of being his babysitter. Never once did I see him do anything that was out of the ordinary. The first time I knew that my husband ever drank at all was the night we got married. First off, he was an hour late to our wedding – not a big fancy one, just in front of a minister with no guests. "We had a small reception afterward with friends and family. During the course of the reception, my older stepsister and her husband (who was an alcoholic also) felt it a fun thing to do to get my husband plastered, and plastered he was.

It ruined my whole honeymoon. He remained drunk all night long. He had an obsession that his ex-wife had been cheating on him and had her boy-friends hidden in the house. So the first night of our marriage, he confused me for her and continually called me by her name, dragged me through the house by my hair and my arm, looked under beds and in closets, and slammed me against the walls of the house, demanding to know where I hid my boyfriend. The next morning he apologized, and I forgave him, thinking it was but a fluke.

This was very wrong, and it was only the beginning. I was married to him for six and a half years. One year into the marriage, I gave my heart to Jesus. That decision came when a door-to-door Tupperware sales woman tried to sell me a glass. This same woman would be my friend for years to come. I was such a baby Christian then. I was raised in a church all my life and went to parochial school, but it was only a way of life to me, *not the way* of life. There is a big difference.

The first two years of marriage, we lived in the house his first wife and he shared. I became friends with the neighbor lady. She worked nights, and so did my husband. Her husband would get mine drunk, and he would still go to work. The neighbor's husband kept making passes at me. I was so scared to go around there, so I stayed away unless the wife was home. Later on, after we were married, I found out then that he had been toeing the mark so he could keep the girls permanently. Once he had the final custody papers in his hands, then and only then did his true colors come out.

He ended up being an alcoholic and turned to drinking. My life was hell all over again! He was a violent drunk. Perhaps I had been drawn to him by the unconscious thing inside of me that said, "If you love me, you will beat me, and if you don't beat me, you don't love me." Whenever someone said to me that they loved me as a child, I got beat. This is called a conditioned reflex.

One day I was so sick, so I went to the doctor. I thought I had the flu that was going around and couldn't keep anything down. The doctor examined me and said, "The bad news is that you do not have the flu, and the good news is that you are pregnant." I was in shock.

I went home and told my husband. He was glad at the news, but I still had to work. Three months later they did an ultrasound and told me I had not one baby but two inside of me. About six months into the pregnancy, I found myself running into problems. The babies were turning in such a way that they were kicking my heart and causing extra heart beats, which made me pass out. I ended up being taken by taxi to the hospital from work. I remained there for a week before I was finally able to come home. I was placed on bed rest and was under doctor's orders to start maternity leave.

My husband was drinking one night, and he came home angry and punched me in the stomach. We didn't know it then, but his punch killed one of the babies in the womb. No one knew about him punching me because I kept my mouth shut. I didn't want him to go to jail, so I remained silent, as I always did when pain was inflicted on me. I learned early on that to tell the truth was stupid because no one believed you anyhow.

At any rate, I delivered at the beginning of the seventh month, and my son was born. He was an identical twin, but the other one had decayed inside the womb, and my son had to survive the poison in the womb. He was born dead, and they revived him. He was twelve inches long and weighed two pounds. He had blond hair, but I couldn't tell what color eyes he had, as only the whites showed. His pupils and irises were down in the sockets, hidden by his cheekbones. They thought he had been born blind. His feet were backward and his legs twisted. They said he would die also, but I knew in my heart he would not die. Once again, I talked to this Jesus, and once again, he appeared to me and told me my son would live. And I believed him. Mind you, I had no relationship with Jesus, except he kept coming into my life periodically and talking to me, reassuring me that he was there and I would learn later on what was happening to me and why he was there. I just knew he was. Certainly, I didn't understand, but I felt peace in talking to him.

My son survived. It took three months before they allowed him to come home with me. His being home did not stop my husband from drinking. I went back to work after maternity leave and worked another year. When my son was eight months old and being babysat by a neighbor lady, I got called into the commanding officer's conference room, where he told me to get my things and go home, as my house was on fire. Needless to say, I panicked. When I got home, I found out I had lost everything I had. My husband had been drinking and decided he needed to take the carpeting off the kitchen floor. He did not put out the pilot lights on the stove, nor did he bother to shut off the gas. He did remember to blow out the pilot lights on the stove, but that let gas fumes into the house. When he poured gasoline on the carpet to loosen it from the cement flooring beneath it, the fumes built up and blew my home up, destroying everything I had. It was a mess.

I learned from that fire that when fiberglass curtains are heated in the flames of a fire, a chemical combustion happens, and they disintegrate and become part of the smoke. The smoke and melting fiberglass come together and form fiberglass cobwebs from ceiling to floor and from wall to wall. My home was a total disaster. I cried for a long time over that one. The household insurance rebuilt the inside, but I had lost things that I could never replace.

It was about this time that I met my husband's ex-wife and saw how much she wanted to see her daughters and heard how he had lied to the judge, saying he didn't know where she was and then saying to her that he didn't know when the divorce was to be heard. Obviously, he got custody through deceit. My husband's ex-wife had remarried a man with five children, and they were happy together. He was a Baptist and knew the Lord. My husband's ex-wife had found God, gotten baptized, and was saved. Remember, I came from a background where I yearned to have a real mother and never had that privilege. I wanted the girls to have their mother, so I befriended the ex-wife and would sneak the girls over to see their mother while their dad was at work.

When my son was about a year old, my husband got drunk again, and once again, he set the house on fire, the second time in one year. He fell asleep in bed with a lit cigarette in his hands. His bed caught on fire, and the curtains were next, and then he was on the floor, burning. I had taken the kids to the store to get some food. And came home to find the house on fire. I had enough. I made the kids stay in the car while I ran next door and woke up the neighbors. They called the fire department and police. The firefighters came and put out the fire. I called his ex-wife and told her to come and get the girls so they didn't have to live that way.

She came with the police, got her girls, and got custody of them right then and there. As she was leaving with the girls, I grabbed my son and was leaving also. I wasn't going to stick around anymore. He started begging her to not take the girls. She told him he should be begging me to stay, as I was going out the door with his son. He took his wedding band off, threw it at me, and told her he didn't care about me or his son. He was only concerned about her and the girls.

She left with the girls, and as I was climbing in my car, she came over and told me to follow her to her house. When I got there, she told me, as did her husband, that my son and I were to stay with them and that we could have the rooms in their basement until I could get on my feet. And so I did. My son and I lived with his ex-wife and her new husband and children. I filed for divorce and would have divorced him, but he came crying and begging, and I gave in and took him back. Big mistake, but I took him back.

He literally traded the house that burned down (after it was once again fixed up by the insurance people) with a family in another town "even Steven" for their home. So we moved to another home in another town and were going to shoot for fresh beginnings. He did not get his girls back right away. They stayed with their mom. Eventually, they came back and lived with us again. The girls were returned to his custody by their choice. I loved the girls, and they loved me. They had two mothers who loved them, and we worked together for their good. I didn't want them to ever have to experience the hurt and torment that I had gone through.

The girls were starting their puberty years. They were in the latter years of grade school. Their daddy (my husband) worked at a factory and made big money, but he drank it all up. In order to buy the girls and my son clothes, shoes, etc., I had to clean houses during the day to make extra money. I managed to do just that, but there was not money left over for school lunches. I talked to the principal at the school, and the girls were allowed to have free breakfast and lunches. But this was embarrassing to them, and they resented their dad because of it. I remember one day, one of the twins came to me and asked if there was any way I could get her a pair of shoes. The kids were tormenting her because she had shoes that had holes in them and her toes were showing through her sneakers. So I cleaned an extra house that week, and when they came home from school, there were new shoes and clothes on the beds for them all. They thought Christmas had come early. I'll never forget their faces when they saw the new things – not hand-me-downs, but new things.

The drinking went on, and life became worse. He became more and more violent. One night we decided to go get pizza with the kids, only we didn't know there was an ice storm. Well, I went out the door first, hit an ice patch, went up in the air, and fell on my back down three concrete steps on our porch, each step breaking a spot in my back. He got me up and laid me on the living room couch. I couldn't move or get up on my own because my back was broken. That canceled the trip to get pizza.

I lay on that couch for two weeks, unable to get up. He hated doctors and refused to take any of us to see one. All he would do was torment me and call me ugly names and lazy because I wasn't cleaning his home or doing his laundry. He told me all I wanted to do was lay on the couch. There was no way to call anyone for help, as the phone was in the next room. I laid there for two weeks in absolute pain every time I tried to move. At the end of the two weeks, I was able to get up. Although I was bent over and still in severe pain, I walked next door and begged the neighbor to take me to the doctor's office. She did. My husband never knew this, as he was at work, the girls were in school, and she watched the baby for me while I was there.

The doctor saw me and sent me over for X-rays. When they got done, the technician came out and touched one of the broken places in my back and asked, "Does this hurt?" It hurt so bad that I screamed and fell to the floor. They came with a stretcher and carried me to a room. He called the doctor's office and told him that I had broken my back in three places. The doctor told them to admit me, and then he came over to the hospital and talked to me privately. He wasn't too fond of my husband. Boy he was mad! By this time my husband was home from work, wondering where I was.

Well, let me tell you, that doctor got on the phone and told him he had exactly half an hour to pack a bag for me, bring it to the hospital, and that he'd better cooperate with treatment for me or he would sign papers and have him arrested. Needless to say, my husband had that bag packed and came to the hospital. I don't know what the doctor said to him in private, but he sure was good to me for a while.

Another time, the oldest twin (now in junior high) had been hit in the head by a volley ball at school, and she came home with a headache. I knew she had a concussion, but her daddy wouldn't let me take her to the doctor. He insisted she go to school the next morning. I put her on the bus and sent her, and he went off to work. After he went to work, I called the school and told them I suspected she had a concussion, and I would not be responsible for her at school, as her daddy was the one that made her come and refused her medical treatment. They had me come and get her right away. They didn't want the responsibility of her injury either. So I picked her up from school and took her to the doctor, and sure enough, she had a concussion. I kept her home for a few days until the doctor said she could go back to school. Seems I was always fighting with him for the sake of the kids and myself.

I didn't believe in divorce, as I had read in the Bible where God didn't like divorce. Yet I could not reconcile myself to the fact that God would want me to be a punching bag either. So I prayed, "Lord, you show me. Give me a sign, and I will stay longer." Each time I prayed, it got worse at home. Five years into the marriage, he still didn't know my name. He continued to call me by his first wife's name. If anything happened with the girls or he wanted to change something in his home, he would call his ex, and they would make the decisions on how to change things and how to discipline the girls. This gave the girls, who were impressionable at that time, the idea they didn't have to listen to me anymore. And they didn't. It was an awful time for me. I was trying to honor my marriage vow before God and still couldn't reconcile how things were in my life as being godly. Finally, I realized that it was okay for me to leave this marriage. And I did.

I was scared of him at that point and felt the only way I could get out of the marriage was to sell things and get a car of my own. I certainly wouldn't take his car, even though he had two. So I sold, worked, and saved and finally had enough money to leave. One day he went to work, the girls went to school, and I took my son, my car, our clothes, and a few items that I needed to set up housekeeping again – you know, a mop, broom, dust pan, dishes, household items, and I left. Unbeknownst to me, another neighbor saw me leave and went over after I left and ransacked his house. When they came home, the appliances, bedroom sets, everything was gone. Of course I got the blame, and to this day, he still believes I did all of that.

I left and went to the state where my natural mother lived. I rented a mobile home, placed my son in kindergarten down there, and took a job in a nursing home. Remember, I had an inward conditioning that was not apparent to me yet. I was seeking subconsciously those who would hurt me instead of walking free because of all that happened to me as a child.

I wasn't there long, and I met a man who appeared to be nice. We dated, and I began to trust him, even loaning him my car sometimes while I was at work. My parents watched my son for me. It turned out this guy was a drug runner for a major drug cartel in the country and he was running drugs in my car. One night the police were chasing him, and he threw the drugs into the river out the window of my car and smacked the side of a bridge, denting my car. That is when I got him to tell me what he really was doing. But after confronting him, he told me that he had my trailer rigged with a hidden bomb and if I opened my mouth, he would just blow me and my son up while we slept one night. Needless to say, I was scared to death.

I didn't know it at the time, but he was being tailed by the FBI. One night while I was at work in the nursing home, three gentlemen came to see me. I was taken into an office, and each identified themselves as FBI and showed me their IDs. They said if I cooperated with them, no one would know I was involved. They could tell I was scared. So I told them what I knew and how he said that my trailer was wired. They said they would protect me and watch me, my son, and my parents so none of us would get hurt. They wanted me to hang in there with him for a while and see what I could find out. So I did.

They had a good case on him, and they were closing in when he took off to Hawaii. He was eventually traced there, but somehow the cartel turned on him, and I heard they slaughtered him and scattered his parts all across the mountains of Hawaii. They found enough to identify the body and tell his mother, who was a school teacher back in my mom's state. They searched my trailer and found that there was no bomb. They released me of any involvement because I was just one of his victims.

Shortly after this happened, my husband, (I wasn't divorced yet) my son's father, discovered where I was and turned in a false abuse report accusing me of torturing my son and starving him. The authorities had to investigate. As God would have it, I had just bought groceries the day before and had my pantries and my refrigerator full. They showed up at my door one night after I returned from picking my son up from school. They examined him and found no bruises, and my son told them I never hit him but I gave him time out. They searched my refrigerator and my cabinets and found plenty of food, so they knew he wasn't doing without food. His clothes were washed and cleaned, and the trailer was spotless. So they deemed it a false report by a mad ex-husband. Unfortunately, they reported back to my soon-to-be ex's state and gave the exact location of where I lived.

He hired a lawyer and forced me back to that state so a divorce could be done. I got full custody of my son with him having visitation rights, but he didn't come to see him for a while. He was always too drunk to come. Later on he would come faithfully. I will say this about him though: he never missed a child support payment, and it was always on time. For that I was grateful.

Coming back for the divorce hearing, I had to quit my job where I was and look not only for a place to live but a job. When I finally got back there with my belongings, I only had seventy-five dollars to my name. I found a nice small apartment downtown on what we called "the strip" right next to a tavern. They never bothered us any. The exact cost was seventy-five dollars per month. It was right across the street from the Salvation Army. The girl in the office there helped me with utilities, and we became friends. She would always stop after work and make sure we were all right. I made a home out of it.

I found a church there and they helped me out a lot. I became actively involved in the church. I eventually became a bus pastor, which meant I commanded a bus and its driver, and every Sunday we traveled the inner city and picked up kids and parents and took them to church. I visited all these homes on Saturdays, and then come Sunday I would go back and bring them to church and Sunday school. I ran 176 kids every Sunday to school. God bless that small ministry.

Did I stay in God's will? No! I fell and I walked away from all of it. You have read that I wove in and out of Christianity for several years, and each time it was a lesson learned and a healing process for me. I was sincere in giving my heart to the Lord but immature at how to stay a Christian. My immaturity and the wounds of the past would trip me up every time. Our enemy, the devil, knew exactly where to strike. It was almost like a snake that bites over and over again until you realize the snake is dangerous and can bring death to you. It did bring death to me as a Christian. Yet God, in *his* infinite mercy, kept coming and reaching out to me. He never once let me stay on the wrong path. He always found me and brought me back to him.

GOING FORWARD ...
OR SO I THOUGHT

I was now living downtown on the strip, as they called it – land of the hooker's and pimps. There were adult bookstores on just about every corner. The local "in" thing for teens to do was to ride the one ways (the downtown area consisted of two one way streets), so they made a loop cruising the town every night. There were the teens, and there were the adults, and then there were those that frequented the porn buildings and, every so often, a tavern. A tavern was what my apartment complex was right next to. You would think they would be loud and rowdy, but this one wasn't as bad, and the owner had his bouncers look out for my place, as he knew I was a single woman with a small child and the next door neighbor was an elderly lady.

The elderly lady was known in the neighborhood as the Big Grouch. No one wanted anything to do with her, as she was mean, spiteful, and very hateful. Well, my son was five years old then and didn't know a stranger. Every day when he came home from kindergarten, he would go next door and knock on this old lady's door and offer her an apple.

At first she growled and declined, but when it became obvious that he would not go away and would always show up, she started to mellow and actually started to smile, laugh, and look forward to that time in the evening. The three of us would sit out back and just chat and laugh. It turned out she was just lonely and scared.

While I was living there, there was a knock on my front door one Saturday morning. It was some people inviting us to come to their church. They said they would pick us up in a bus on Sunday mornings and evenings. We decided to try this church out. I was once again reaching out to God and Jesus; still making my way into a closer relationship with him and yet not knowing how to go about it. Well, we went and we loved it! So we started going every Sunday.

My son went to the children's church, and I went to the adult services. Our bus pastors (as they were called back then) had a route in the inner city. It consisted of a married couple and the bus driver. The more I went, the more I got on fire for the Lord. And the more I rode the bus, the more the driver and I talked. One day he asked me to dinner and I went. That was the beginning of a courtship. He seemed to be an upstanding man and a pillar in the church. He was always talked about from the pulpit by the pastor as being faithful and having been the one who started the bus ministry. One thing led to another, and soon our courtship ended in marriage.

Oh, I was happy! I had the Lord, I was married to a good Christian man, and he was teaching me the bus ministry. I became involved with the bus ministry, the youth ministry, and the helps ministry (helping to run the clothing and food ministry out of the church). I was a go-getter for the Lord! My heart was that I was doing it for the Lord, and I enjoyed helping others very much and still do, for that matter.

The pastor and two associate pastors in the church took turns speaking. The main pastor was great. He built the church from sixty-eight people to 3,000 per service. It was the Lord who blessed him and gave him favor with the people. He ministered to the people in true agape love. They knew he loved them, and they did whatever it took to make the church run smoothly.

After my husband and I had been married a while, one of the co-pastors suddenly left the church. The main pastor told the congregation that he had been offered a pastoral job elsewhere and decided to accept the position. They gave him a going-away party and sent him and his wife to their new destination.

The pastor, who had become friends with my husband and I, asked us if we could take in a sixteen-year-old boy and give him a home. We said yes because he was a worker on our bus each week. The young man moved in with us, and for a season, I had two sons. But then the boy started acting funny and avoiding me.

One evening, my husband of three years came home and threw his stuff in blanket on the bed and picked up the corners and made a bag – something like you see Santa Claus carry in the books – and he said good-bye. He just walked out the door as if nothing meant a thing to him – no explanation or anything. I had always wondered why the marriage had never been consummated, yet I honored my marriage vows and never cheated on him at all.

That same evening I noticed the young man who was staying with us also did not come home. The next day I was called into the pastor's office, and he was forced to admit something to me – something he knew before he married us and never once said a word to me about. At any rate, the young man I had in my home (mind you, this same pastor had asked me to take him in) happened to be the cause for my disappearing husband's first marriage ending. I guess his first wife came home and caught him in bed with this young man in a compromising position. Had I been told the truth, I never would have married this man, nor would I have taken this young man into my home.

It turns out my husband had married me as a closet homosexual who wanted to appear normal by marrying me. He used me to cover his own actions. In the end, I found out he ran away with this young man to California – where same-sex marriages were allowed – and married this young man. I was devastated. I saw a lawyer, and they annulled the marriage and erased it off the books. I spent three years in a marriage that was no marriage and didn't count as one in the end.

I felt betrayed by the church, by the pastor, and by all who knew it and did not say a word. I don't know if it was the confidentiality thing, but to me it would have been better to have warned me than to let me walk through this lifestyle and be as hurt as I was. I was angry, bitter, and hurt by the pastor of the church because I felt in my heart he had betrayed me and lied to me. He told me he was sorry. I left the church and entire ministry for several years. I no longer trusted pastors or ministries or churches at that point in time.

It was about five years before I decided to go back to church. It was like God would never let go of me. Oh, I think I always believed in God, but for now I was wandering, hurt, angry, and bitter. I didn't walk from churches and ministry; I ran from them! But you can't outrun the Lord.

After five years, I ran into the assistant pastor who had left the other church, and he told me he had returned to the area, as it didn't work out. He had started another church of his own, and he invited me to go there. It took him some time to convince me to go. By then I was renting an apartment in the middle of town. I really wasn't that far from his church. Finally, I agreed to go. Once again, I took my son and went back to church.

I enjoyed it, enjoyed the people there and the preaching. I got on fire for the Lord, and I became involved. Faithfully, I would come and clean the church every week. I enjoyed doing it, as it was time alone with God and I could talk to him. My joy with church and pastors and ministry was about to come to a screeching halt once again.

The pastor came in one evening when I was cleaning. I sort of ignored him and let him do his thing while I did my work. The building had a basement, a main floor, and an upstairs, and I cleaned them all. I thought the pastor had gone from the building and gone home. I had the key, and it was not unusual for me to lock up when I cleaned. But boy did I get a surprise that night.

As I came downstairs and turned the corner from the stairwell, there sat the pastor completely naked, with his clothes on the floor. I froze, I honestly didn't know what to do. I was shocked, to say the least, and scared. Remember the background that I grew up in with the sexual abuse of my grandfather and father. I just froze. That gave the man the leverage he needed. He crossed the room, took me upstairs, laid me on the altar of the church, and raped me. I didn't scream. I didn't fight. I just lay there. I didn't know what to do. Who was going to believe me if I told them what the pastor had done? Also, if he could do this to me, could he not kill me, if he so desired? These were the thoughts going through my mind.

I never said a word about it to anyone. It was the beginning of another nightmare for me. He would try to get me alone, and sometimes he did, no matter how much I tried to avoid him. I quit cleaning the church, gave back my key, and I left. It was then that women from the church started coming to me, some with marital problems and some single women. They all told me the same thing. They didn't know who to go to, but they wanted me to know this pastor was raping them and stalking them. I was a victim of his rapes, and yet I was the one who was counseling them and helping them to deal with it. And yet I couldn't deal with it myself.

The fact that I had been raped on the altar of the church by the pastor himself made me feel dirty. I felt that I had shamed God and desecrated *his* church, *his* sanctuary. I just couldn't bring myself to enter a church or be alone with a male pastor for a long, long time.

The elders of the church were friends of mine. I was at their home one evening, and they were talking about the church. One of the elders said he didn't understand what was going on, but every time he had to stand by the pastor, he got physically ill and had to go throw up. I told him I knew why it was happening. When he asked me why, I asked him if he would believe me if I told him the truth. He said yes, and that was the first time I said a word about what the pastor had done to me and why I left the church. I told him of the seven women in the church who came to me and why they were all quitting the church too.

He called a meeting of the elders. They met in a home and decided they would handle it the biblical way. So they set up a church court hearing. Each of the women, including myself, was brought in the room one at a time, and we told our story of how he raped us. It was a nightmare, for they not only had the elders in there, but they had every male member of the church. The only other woman in the room was the pastor's wife.

The pastor's wife demanded to know if I saw his birthmark and where it was. I told her I was being raped; I didn't look for birthmarks. I just stared into space. They were all asking how long it took. Who carries a stop watch when they are being raped? They were of the mentality that I was either making it all up or I deserved what I got. Yet they couldn't deny the stories of seven women all saying the same thing individually without knowing what the other was saying. One of the elders was a cop. He had worked with rape cases and knew we were telling the truth (or so I thought).

In the end, all seven of us women were banned from the church, and the pastor was kept on. God directed me to tell the pastor that within a short period of time the church would be scattered and he would be gone from the area. True to the word of God, the church was disbanded, and the members scattered. Many never did return to the Lord, and their souls were lost.

Shortly after this, I ran into the secretary of the other church that he had co-pastored. She let it slip that this same pastor who had just raped all of us had been guilty of that clear back in that church. He had not been called elsewhere to minister but had been kicked out by the other pastor and his board of directors for raping the women there. And upon their investigation, they learned this raping pastor had done the very same thing in five other churches. Never once did any of them press charges.

I don't know where he went or what he is going now, but I sincerely pray he found the Lord and is not harming the sheep anymore. His answer to it all was that God had called him to be the shepherd of the flock, and as shepherd of the flock, he was to meet every need of the flock, including the sexual needs of the women doing without. Not!

Then I really went bonkers. This was the second minister in a row who had harmed me rather than helped me, and both of them quenched my spirit. I did not want to serve a God who did these things. I lashed out at God and at churches, and I went out into the world. I met a man in the world and ended up married to him.

We got married in November, and in mid-December I got a phone call from his mom asking for him. I told her he was at work, and she asked who I was. I said I was his wife, and she said I couldn't be. When I asked why not, she told me his wife and three kids were standing next to her. Well, *shocked* is not the word for it. I was wife number two in two states.

With this phone call, wife number one found out about me, and she started divorce proceedings. At the same time I found out about her, my marriage was annulled because it didn't legally exist. By the time we both got done with our legal proceedings against him, he had a third wife in a third state. I was glad to have found out, but now I hated men to boot.

Deep down I probably hated men anyhow because of all I went through as a child. Every time I started to trust men, I got socked a good one and ended up being the hurt one. You see, it was a vicious circle. I didn't know that I was subconsciously attaching myself to men who would hurt me. Growing up, anytime someone said, "I love you," they hurt me in one fashion or another. I was like the lab rat that did not eat unless the light turned on. That is how I gauged my relationships with men subconsciously. If you love me, then hurt me, or you really don't love me. To love something was to get hurt.

Now I was on a dead run from the Lord. I was never going to set foot in a church again. I was never going to be hurt like that again. I just could not go into a church anymore because after being raped on the altar of the church, I felt that God had to hate me for having sex in *his* church and on the altar, and even more so from *his* minister or leader. I felt if I stepped inside a church again, God would strike me dead. I just didn't believe that God wanted anything to do with me. I felt dirty and ugly, and I started to hate myself. It would be a while before I learned what love was truly about. But then that is yet another chapter.

THE MERRY-GO-ROUND

*B*y now you probably realize that I was on a merry-go-round going nowhere but in circles. I would subconsciously seek out only those men and those people who would abuse me all in the name of love. I became worse than the conditioned scientific mouse that only ate when the light came on. I didn't realize I was that way. To say you love me meant you would inflict some sort of deep hurt into my physical body or my life or you just plain didn't love me.

I survived the ordeal of being raped by the pastor of the church on the altar. I survived the church court done all in the name of the Lord. I learned that there was no justice in the man-made and man-run house of the Lord. I learned once again to never tell the truth, as it only brought me heartache and pain. There were no words to describe the pain in my heart or my spirit after all of this.

If you dared to ask me to church, I would run as fast as I could in the opposite direction. I would not look back, and I would never talk to you again. You immediately became my enemy. I was driven by fear and shame. For a long time, if I so much as looked at a church, I trembled inside and broke out in a cold sweat. I was too scared to even enter a church, not only because of the fear of it happening again but the fear that God would strike me dead on the spot.

Oh, I loved the Lord. I truly did. But all that happened to me caused me to walk in such shame. I felt dirty. I felt like even God didn't want me, as I had desecrated *his* house, *his* church! I couldn't even pray. How could I talk to God when I had just had sex on the altar of *his* church! And not one of the people from that church body – not even those elders who believed me – reached out to me or even once said they cared what happened to me. Looking back now, I suppose they were shocked it happened at all and also didn't know how to handle it. So it was easier to walk away and pretend it didn't happen.

I struggled with the shame and guilt for a long time. I wandered away from God, and I just figured there was no longer any hope for me. So I tried to go out in the world and live it as if there was no tomorrow. I got wrapped up in drinking and partying and occasional sex – not prostitution, just occasional sex with whomever. Not that I wanted it, but it was my way of getting back at men for all the hurt they had inflicted on me through the years. For a season I used my body to "love 'em and leave 'em." I didn't care as long as I hurt them like all the men had hurt me. It was my own personal revenge, I guess. I no longer had to worry about repercussions from God. I was so convinced he didn't care anyhow, not after the incident at the church. After all I had made a mess of *his* church and violated the holiness of *his* home – the church!

While I was out running around and hurting men, I ran into this man who stuck it out with me. I eventually agreed to marry him. Heck, why not settle down and try to make some sense of my life? Well, I married him all right – for one month. It was annulled after one month, as he already had a wife. My marriage was *not* legal. So actually I couldn't and wasn't married to the man. She divorced him. I annulled him, and he married a third time before the divorce and annulment could go through. So actually I was married to a bigamist. Geesh, would I never learn? But then, why bother? I couldn't go to God. The shame and anger was too deep and too much for me to confront and I couldn't deal with it.

It was about this time that I ran into another lady who just wouldn't leave me alone. I kept telling her to leave me alone, but she came around and just kept telling me that she loved me but, more importantly, Jesus loved me. I wanted to hit her so bad but never did. I just ran the other way. The only trouble was I couldn't shake this one. She told me I had to come to her church and visit. I fought it. I told her I didn't want to, that I hated pastors and all men. She told me that her pastor was a woman. She kept at me and kept at me, and finally, out of the idea that if I went one time she would leave me alone, I went to her church. Well, I went, but boy my heart was pounding as soon as I came to the door of the church. I broke out in a cold sweat. I forced myself to go in the doors because it was the only way to shut this woman up and make her leave me alone.

I sat and I listened, but my heart was pounding so loud I figured it could be heard a block away. Something happened in there. The Holy Spirit showed up, and somehow I found myself up front at the altar, and that woman pastor was praying for me.

I knew she hadn't seen me ever before, and yet she told me that God loved me and that Jesus died for me and that there was no sin too big that he did *not* and would *not* forgive. Inside, I'm saying, *Yeah, right lady. You just don't know.* I started shaking from head to toe, and the next thing I knew, I was picking myself up off the floor, and they told me I had been "slain in the spirit." I thought I just fainted, buy they explained it all. I accepted their explanation, and the shaking and the cold sweat were gone. I guess God just figured that I had endured enough shame, guilt, and sorrow and did not expose me. Up until now no one has known these things, except those directly involved.

I felt so relieved. I wept for a long time. I just couldn't stop. There is no way I can describe the depth of shame I felt, but every time I hear the song "The Alabaster Box," I cry because I know the shame Mary Magdalene felt as she walked through the jeering crowds to present her alabaster box to Jesus.

Once again I became on fire for the Lord. I got involved once again. I reached out to others. I was like a sponge soaking up water. I couldn't get enough of this Jesus. I knew what it was like to wear filthy rags, and suddenly go through a spiritual cleansing, and to shake off the old man. I felt so much freedom.

It was during this time that I realized what an intercessor was and that God was using me to intercede for others. I was part of the pastor's intercessory prayer team. She would call us together, tell us what was going on, and then we would all pray faithfully. We trusted her and were faithful. But we found out later that she did not trust us. She was holding out on us.

It seems that her son was bound up in drugs, and she struggled with this problem, never once asking us to hold her up in prayer for her or her son. One night her son bought some cocaine on the street. He thought it was the pure stuff. What he didn't know was it was laced with pure arsenic, and he snorted a whole lot of it. He became violently ill. To make a long story short, he died in her arms. It was only then that the rest of us found out.

As intercessors, we were shocked that she never let us know and had not trusted us enough to have us cover this problem in prayer. I guess she felt that pastors were not to let any of the sheep know they were human and had problems. After finding out, the intercessors grouped together, trying to help each other understand why she didn't trust us with her situation. We began to wonder if she truly trusted us at all and what else she had kept from us. We were wounded and hurt, and we were truly seeking answers and closure.

Well, there was an Evangelist who also stood in the office of a prophet who had ministered many times in her church. Out of the blue, he showed up in town and sought us out. He called a meeting, which later became several meetings. He said God sent him to us to minister to us, and he rallied us back into the intercessors we were supposed to be. We were not having secret meetings to undermine the church or the leadership or the ministry. We were being ministered to individually and corporately and being set back on track by the true man of God. The only problem was that the enemy was still working through the pastor who lost her son. She found out about the meetings and called us into her office. She raked us over the coals and told us we were not being loyal to her.

In our hearts and minds, we had been ministered to by this prophet of the Lord to the point we knew we had to be loyal to God, not a person and not to a minister. She blamed the prophet and said he was backstabbing her, though he wasn't. We all tried to explain, but there was no explaining to her. She banned him from ministering in her church ever again. This action hurt us all over again. Most of us, including me, left the church and never went back.

Once again I was hurt inside the church. It seemed that each time I went forward and got on fire, I got wounded by the pastor and leadership. I loved God but sure didn't want anything to do with church. I felt they were all hypocrites. They were following after man and *not* God. They didn't care how many sheep they wounded as long as they got their way.

So, again, I wandered away. I stayed away from churches for a long, long time. I didn't want anyone to even talk to me about church. After a while of being away, I just lost interest, and the fire in me shut down. Spiritually, I waxed cold. I ceased to even read the Bible or think about God. I had enough. I just threw my hands up and quit.

ONCE AGAIN

I was once again out, wounded and running from God. All my life I had been working toward this relationship with the man I occasionally saw and talked to in visions. And I just never could find him to get understanding or someone who could tell me what was happening. The only true happiness I knew was when I was with him and having conversations. There were times when my darkest moments would consume me and I would sit on the floor or on my bed or in a chair and just talk as if he was sitting right there in front of me or beside me. I would pour my heart out to him, and when I was done, a sensation of warmth would go all over me and through me. Such peace would consume me. I didn't realize then that he *did* hear every word that I spoke, even though I was not aware of *his* presence.

In the world's eyes, I probably would have been locked up for being crazy talking to nothing but thin air. All I knew was that these moments were peaceful ones to me and that I just felt the need to sit down and chat awhile. I didn't truly understand what was taking place, but my spirit-man did. It always accepted the peace that I received in these moments as reality – no questions, just reality.

God was always sending people to cross my path who took me one step further that he wanted me to take. This time it was a woman I met in a grocery store. She said hi, and one thing led to another, and soon this lady invited me to her church. I didn't promise her that I would go but ended up going anyhow. It turned out they had a guest speaker that Sunday, and she was named Amy Grant. Once again I was pulled back into a church setting, and once again a fire was relit, and once again I started to get involved.

It was here that I became involved in their shelter for abused women and children. I ended up helping out there and taking a shift. It was here that God started using me in the gifts of the Holy Spirit or they started manifesting in me. There was a lounge just off the laundry room. We would sit around and talk at night while the laundry was being done. God started showing me things about them and giving me words for them. I would pray for them, not realizing yet too much about laying on of hands and praying. It was here that I first prayed for a woman, and she was slain in the spirit. After that, the women would come and be ministered to, and it became a time with the Lord where they could lay their burdens down. They came in wounded and hurt and left whole and rejoicing.

However, it didn't take long for jealousy to set in. The "higher-ups" in the church did not have these gifts operating in them. So I was asked to stop. It happened time and time again after they asked me to stop. They forgot to ask God to stop. He just showed up and things happened. Needless to say, I was asked to leave. I spent two years there ministering to those women and children, and I know they were changed and set free. For he whom the Lord has set free is free indeed!

How can I go in and out so much? One moment I was on fire for God and the next moment running from God. I don't know how to answer that question except to say, when you build a fire in the fireplace, sometimes an ember gets separated from the rest of the group. It glows for a season and then starts to die. When noticed by the keeper of the fire, the ember is pushed back into the pile with the rest, and before long they are just as hot and on fire as the rest of the embers. This is the best way I can describe what was happening to me.

So once again I went off by myself. It seemed to me that churches were good for using me to their gain, but when I needed something, they weren't around. Oh, this is not true of all churches, but in some, it certainly is true. I wasn't rich. I didn't have a high-paying job. I was, in fact, what I refer to as a "throw-away Christian." It didn't matter whether I was there or not as long as the church leaders got the glory. God will not share *his* glory with any man!

I started rambling through life again. I stayed to myself and continued to raise my son. I joined another church. Remember, there was this drive in me to meet this One I talked to on a daily basis, the One who loved me unconditionally. But nowhere was I truly finding him. In reality I didn't know it was him who I sought to begin with.

I met a man and wife ministry team who were Quakers. They reached out to me and invited me to their church. So I went. They were struggling with a hurting church. There was something that drew me to them. I started attending their church on a regular basis and went to their Bible studies. One day they got on the subject of the Holy Spirit gifts, and come to find out, they were both spirit-filled and struggling to teach their church. But teach they did.

It was also a time that I met yet another man. Remember, I was *not* a committed Christian yet. I was still taking a walk, seeking the One I talked to all the time and doing more stumbling than walking. At any rate, this man I met was gentle, kind, and broke through the wall of stone around my heart. I was seeking love and acceptance but in all the wrong places. He eventually proposed to me, and I agreed to marry him. I asked my Quaker pastor to marry us, and he said he would.

Everything was set up; we were to be married in a neighbor's living room. Just before the wedding, the man came over, and I guess he was so sure of himself that he showed his true character, or at least the beginnings of it. He got upset with me and pulled a dresser drawer out and threw it at me. It missed me, but nonetheless, he threw it at me. It was then I heard this voice speak audibly to me and say, "Don't do it. Don't marry him." Well, I had not been delivered from hate of men yet, and I disobeyed the voice that just spoke to me. That was when I learned the hard way what happens when you disobey God: you reap your disobedience and all the things that go with it.

I went through with the marriage. I became pregnant and lost them in the fourth month of pregnancy. I say lost *them* because I was carrying five at the time. I was prone to multiple births naturally. I became pregnant again. I started having trouble with the pregnancy in the eighth month, so I was transported one hundred miles away. This left my young son at the mercy of my husband because I had disobeyed and married. You see, God saw what I could not, and I was soon to learn the truth.

I didn't know this, but he was deep in pornography. It was something he hid, but it got such a hold on him that while I was in the hospital trying to save our baby's life, he was home with my son. When he did it, he told my son that I told him to do it. How could he trick my son into believing this? He would wait until he called me to see how I was doing at the hospital and then would hand up and beat him, telling him I told him to do this on the phone. How sick! My son was a child, scared and alone, and mommy wasn't there to protect him.

I had my own heartache to live through. I went into labor (breech) and was given an epidural, which numbed me, and was set up for C-section. In the middle of the labor, the hospital work shifts changed, so the real doctors went home, and only the interns were on duty, or first-year medical students.

The intern on duty that night refused to listen to me. He had the charts mixed up and took me into the delivery room for a normal delivery. He didn't really know what he was doing, and he cut the umbilical cord with the baby's head still in the womb. That cut the oxygen supply off, and the baby died. The doctor panicked and wrapped the lower torso of the baby's body with a towel and pulled. It tore my insides up and destroyed the baby for good.

I went into immediate surgery for four hours to save my life and then was sent to my room. Needless to say, that doctor is not practicing medicine today. He killed nine babies that night all because he wouldn't listen to the patients and mixed charts up. I was devastated physically and emotionally, and once again I had lost a child.

Certainly, I was in no way prepared for the heartache and anguish that I was to walk through when I returned home from the hospital.

THE WORSE WAS YET TO COME

*T*here was no way that I was prepared for the coming two years of my life, especially for what I was to face and walk through when I got home. I was like a walking zombie. I showed no emotion. I had stitches everywhere, for the doctor had ripped my insides up. I came home to the funeral of my baby son who had been killed by the intern at the hospital. But deal with the funeral I did. I was still in shock, but no one saw that. I was just there.

It was at the funeral that I noticed a strange lady who I had never met before. She was obviously drunk and very upset. I just didn't know who she was or why she was there. I have to admit my curiosity was up, especially when she came up and told me how sorry she was that I had lost my son. Then she hit me with the truth.

She proceeded to tell me that her husband didn't want her there but she had to come. She said she was shocked at my husband. I asked her why, and she said that my husband had told her and her husband that he was a Vietnam War veteran injured in the war and confined to a wheelchair. That was the furthest thing from the truth. I was shocked at this also and was *not* prepared for what she told me next.

She said that she was not part of it but could do nothing, as her husband controlled her and her life. It seems her husband published an underground sex/pornography magazine. My husband had placed an ad in there seeking women for play toys. Oh, how that made me sick to my stomach! However, I was already in shock, so I showed no emotion.

About that time, the funeral director came in and asked if there was anything that he could do for me. I told him yes, that I had a request that was unusual but would appreciate it if he indulged me. I asked him if I could just once hold my baby in my arms and bring closure. I stood there crying, and then he took pity on me. He asked everyone to leave so I could have a private moment. He shut them all out of the room, closed the doors, took my baby out of the casket, and placed him in my arms. For twenty minutes, I held my baby son, and I wept over his body. I needed that, and after a while, I gave my baby back to the funeral director, and he placed my son back in the casket. No one knew what took place but me, God, and the funeral director. To this day I am thankful to him that he took compassion on me and let me hold my baby one time before I had to lay him to rest in the cold ground.

You must be saying, "You have faced enough." No, the worst was yet to come.

I went home after the funeral, and the strange lady called and apologized to me for showing up drunk. She told me she really did care that I lost the baby and she was so sorry but she had to tell me something her husband forbade her to tell. She decided to do it anyhow. She told me that my husband has posted an ad offering me to the highest bidder in the underground sex magazine and had placed my picture and phone number in that magazine advertisement. No wonder I was beginning to get strange phone calls from men I didn't know. Each time I answered, I slammed the received in the caller's ear. I ended up changing my phone number to a private, unlisted one.

It was here that I realized how very much God had spared me while I was in the hospital. Now that I was home, it was all coming out in the open very quickly. I did manage to thank the lady for her honesty, and I told her that God had used her to tell me the truth and that I would be praying for her. Later down the road, because of things I said to her and the compassion of speaking to her decently, she was able to leave her husband, leave that perverted lifestyle, walk out of fear, and accept the Lord.

I was starting to come out of the shock somewhat; not all the way, when I decided to confront my husband. It was then that he started bragging. He boasted that he had been raping five children in the apartment complex we lived in. I later learned he had also raped five women. My head was reeling from all this sickening knowledge. I started to go into shock again, but this time a deep-seated anger arose in me. It wasn't full bloom yet, but the anger took hold of me – a righteous anger. For this was definitely *not* me or anything I wanted a part of, especially having survived my perverted childhood and such.

One day while my husband was gone, I sat my son down, and we had a heart-to-heart talk. My son confessed to me what my husband had been doing to him and how he had accused me of telling him to beat on him. I told my son it was a lie, and he knew I was telling the truth. We went to the authorities and filed a complaint, then returned home. They couldn't find him to arrest him quite yet.

My husband came home later that night, and I confronted him. He laughed in my face. I told him I wasn't scared of him and that I would see him pay for what he did. I said that I had gone to the police and filed charges. He jumped up and plowed me with his fist! I told my son to run for help, and he ran to a neighbor's house, and they called the cops.

When I got off the floor, I called my brother, who was at my dad's house. My brother had just returned from a tour in the army. I told him to come over right away with dad's gun and to make sure it was loaded. My brother did as I asked. Soon, I stood in the hallway with a loaded shotgun pointed at my husband. He ran for the bedroom at the end of the hall. I had my brother call the cops to come get him. I told my husband that if he opened the door, I would shoot him. He knew I would do it, and so did I.

For the first time since I had come home from the hospital, I snapped, and all the rage came out in such hate. I know today if he had come through that door, I would have shot him to death right then and there. But God didn't want me killing anyone. So instead, my husband cut the screen out of the windows in the bedroom and escaped. The police came in about five squad cars. They were everywhere. They finally caught my husband. They had to talk to me and pry my hands off the trigger of the gun. I was going to kill him, as sure as I am breathing today. That is the only time where I felt and experienced the rage that causes one human being to kill another. It was not pleasant and certainly was out of character for me, but all the rage of years of torment was coming out at that moment.

Once he was arrested, he was taken to a psychiatric ward for evaluation, where he was diagnosed as paranoid schizophrenic. He had a dual personality. He never had a twin brother who he had talked about to me several times. He was his own twin brother. That was his alter ego. He was good and bad, but he was never who he said he was. He got off, and they dismissed the charges. Later on he married again and raped his new wife's five kids. To my knowledge, he is now locked up in prison for the rest of his life.

After this happened the police reopened the case where I had filed abuse charges; the state stepped in and took guardianship – not possession of, but guardianship – of my son for two years. We were both court ordered to go to counseling due to the physical and mental trauma that was inflicted on us. Once there, they did not counsel us together but separately. They kept harassing my son to try and make him say I did the abusing and that he was protecting me. My son got fed up and walked out. He told them he was done talking to them, for he had told them the truth that I had nothing to do with it. He refused to go back.

In the times when I went, they tried to play with my mind and get me to say I had beaten my son. I told them that it would be hard to do since I was a patient a hundred miles away at the time of my son's beatings. I was still in shock of all I had walked through from the birth and death of my son, the funeral, the mess with the sex scandal, and now this. I prayed, and God said I was courted ordered to go but not court ordered to talk. So the next session, I told them I had no choice but to show up but would no longer talk to them. Finally, I had enough! I had been pushed to the brink of my mental ability to cope. I walked out and never went back.

I went home and told my son I loved him and together we would make it, but my mind snapped. I locked myself in the bathroom. I had a glass of water in one hand and a full bottle of Valium tranquilizers in the other. I was standing in front of the mirror, and I asked God to forgive me, but I just could not go another step in this life. I had just had all I could bear.

As I looked in the mirror, I didn't see my face. I saw my son standing there, looking at me, and I heard this voice ask me, "What will he do when you are gone? He has no one. He needs you." I saw my son had tears in his eyes. I couldn't stand the pain in his eyes. I put the glass down, put the pills back in the medicine cabinet, and unlocked the door. I went into the bedroom, sat on the floor, laid my head on the side of the bed, and broke for the first time. I sobbed and sobbed and sobbed!

There was a television on the end table behind me, and it was on a channel that had Christian programming. Tammy Faye Baker was there in a close up. I looked into her eyes as she said, "Jesus loves you right where you are." I felt the Holy Spirit, and I knew God was talking to me. He knew exactly where I was, and I turned and cried some more.

I felt something, and I looked up, and there before me was a vision. In this vision was the cross with Jesus hanging on it. He looked awful, almost unrecognizable covered with blood, and he was looking directly down at me. And he was crying!

I asked, "Why are you crying?" He said, "Because I love you and you are hurting." He said, "Look at me," and I did. When I looked, I saw the cross disappear and saw him hang there in glory, covered in a bright light but with a whole body and not a mark on him anywhere. He said, "This is what I have done for you. I took all the pain and bruises and made it all whole again. That is what I want to do for you. I want to make you whole again." He told me he loved me, and I felt warmth go all over my body, and I was at peace.

I asked him, "What should I do?" He told me to go to the county mental health center and ask to speak to one of their counselors. The next day my son and I went there. We spoke to a wonderful woman counselor who interviewed my son and me separately. She heard the same story, so she knew we were telling the truth. She went to bat for us and told me she would do everything in her power to help me keep my sanity in all of this. She realized that I was still a walking zombie and still partially in shock. She went before the judge and pleaded our case. We were taken from state custody and placed in the judge's custody. He ordered a counselor to represent us and assigned us a non-state psychiatrist to come into the home and work for and with us. This all took place, and on one year's time, we were whole, and the court gave me back complete custody of my son. He ordered social services to leave us alone and allow us to heal properly.

Once that was done, I took my son and moved away from the state and into another state. I maintained a job and my home. My son and I became a family. All of this had been left behind.

But this new found peace was *not* to be lone-lived, as I soon was to go on another walk.

HEALING SOME HURTS

I hesitated to start this phase of my book, not because I didn't want to write it, but it is an area where healing was still taking place in my life. I had to deal with some anger that was left in my life, which has disappeared and gone. I had to face some areas I prefer not to remember, as they are fresh in my life, and yet these very hurts have molded me into yet another growth spurt in my life. Know this: we will continue to grow all of our lives here on earth.

We find that our miseries in life are the very things that turn into ministry. For as we come out of our trials and tribulations in life, we can then reach out to others who are still walking in our old shoes and give them hope that one day, as they keep their eyes on Jesus, they too shall wear new shoes, just as I do today.

I was on top of the world. I had just bought a new home, had a new car, and was settling into my first roots in a long time in Iowa. After being in my home for only three weeks, the Lord spoke to me. "I want you to go to Missouri to live by your real mother, stepfather and adopted sister." All I could say was, "But Lord!" Oh, I became a whiner in the worst way. "Why, Lord? Did you not bless me with this new home?" And yet he said to me, "You *are* going."

Now my logical mind is saying, "How am I going to sell this home?" I found out that once God speaks something, it just is. So you might as well stop and listen and do what he says.

In three days' time, without advertising, my home was sold to my satisfaction and the satisfaction of the mortgage holder, and I was on my way to Missouri. After arriving there, I had a home and a job within another three days. God provided *before* I got there.

I should have been happy. "The Lord told me to come here, didn't he?" Little did I know what was to follow? I had some more trials to walk through and some more lessons to learn.

My mom's adopted daughter wanted to go back and get her GED, so I went with her. Yes, I had graduated from high school, but it didn't hurt me to go back with her and learn the updates of schooling, so to speak. It was through her that I met another lady in the class. The lady introduced her brother to my sister, and they arranged for a date.

My adopted sister was shy and insisted that I go with her to meet him before she went on the date, so I did. We met him at his sister's home. He was all dressed up and looked and acted like a gentleman. I remember thinking, *Lord; I'd like a husband like this.* Be careful what you wish for because you just might get it. I did!

Things did not work out with my sister and him, but he came back another time and asked me to go out with him. I agreed to, and I learned that not all is what is seems, but not for years to come. We hit it off, and eventually we decided to get married.

That was the beginning of a long time of heartaches in which I would learn the power of God's provision for me. I went to work, and eventually, we both worked at the same place. It was there that I would be injured for life by getting occupational asthma. It took nine years to finally settle my case and get my worker's comp. My life would never be the same.

During the nine years I waited for things to be right, my husband tried at least three times to have an affair. Each time the woman would eventually come to me and confess, saying they couldn't do that to me because they liked me. I could never have female friends, as he would hit on all of them. Yet I stuck by him because I didn't want another divorce. I hated divorce. Yet I was headed there, only I didn't know it at the time. After the third affair, I told him if I ever caught him again, that would be the end.

He had been married before and had two kids and an ex-wife. The ex and I are still friends to this day. I still have a working relationship with them. They are all Christians. But during the course of the marriage, I would stand in line behind his ex. Always he would rub her in my face. This was not her fault but his. He was the one who did it to me. He would take me on trips where he and his ex had been and then tell me every step of the way what they did. It just took the joy from the trip. After a while, I refused to go on trips with him. I preferred to stay home and just let him go do his thing.

During the nine years of waiting on the worker's comp to be settled, he would torment me, telling me how useless I was because I wasn't working and that I should go to work. My lawyer, my doctors, and the judge said it was impossible for me to work. But he would still rake me over the coals, telling me how useless and lazy I was. When someone tells you negative things about yourself, eventually, you will begin to believe them. But I never went to work, as I couldn't.

I stuck by him, trying to be the wife God intended me to be – for better or worse. The only thing I got was the worst of it. For our fourteenth anniversary, I decided to make a last-ditch effort and surprise him with a honey-moon trip. I forced him into going with me to a weekend getaway. He went, but later I found out that I had ruined a weekend with his secret lover (or at least with one of them). It turned out that he had several going on at once time. Of course, the trip was a dud, and it was miserable. He refused to do anything with me, often taking walks in the area and doing his own thing. So we came home.

One day he went to work, and the Lord told me to turn on his computer. When I did, I found message after message between his girlfriends and him. I read his lies about me and read about all the "wee hour in the morning" phone conversations he was having and about week-end fishing trips that had nothing to do with fishing – weekends when he was supposed to be working and wasn't. What a shock, and yet it was not a shock.

I confronted him, and he left. I found out after he left that he had taken all the money out of the bank. He had sold everything I had stored in my basement and had taken jewelry that my parents had given me and sold it. He kept that money also. He told me he paid the bills, and he hadn't.

I filed for divorce and got it. He skipped and could not be found, so it was me they all came after. Today I struggle with the bills, but God, in one year's time, took me from renting a place to co-owning a home with my son. God has continuously helped me pay my bills. Yes, I still get stressed because of finances, and yet I know that he has made a way, even if I don't see it right now. God has never let me, nor will be ever leave me. He will always meet my needs.

Life has been rough, and life has not been fair, but God has been fair and helped me release the pain of my life and the inner wounds from childhood to now. He has restored much to me. The finances will be the last thing he restores to me. Has it been rough? Yes! Is it rough today? Yes! I have judgments against me in the courts because they can't find him, but they find me. I try to do the right thing and make things right with all concerned. And God has given me favor.

There are things I could share but won't in this book, as some things remain between me and my Lord. One thing I can tell you beyond a shadow of a doubt is that God *is* able and he *will* help you. The things I walked through in my life and am still struggling with, he *will* heal me so that he can continue to touch the lives of the hurting women in this world, giving them hope and causing them to realize that he was with them all along just as he was with me all along.

If he had not been with me, I would not be alive today. I could not write this book and tell you of an awesome God who truly cares for you. Just as *his* unconditional love has been there for me, *his* unconditional love is here for you today. He is the same today, yesterday, and tomorrow. The very things you are walking through today are the very garbage pits that you will help others to climb out of.

No one has to point a finger at me and say, "I know what you did," because I know what I did, and I also know what he did. He reached down and took hold of my hand and held me through every pain and every hurt and every circumstance I walked through. Did I stay with him through it all? No! There were times when I stumbled and times I ran as far away from him as I could. But he never once let go of my hand. He always brought me back and placed my feet on the right path again. Through every hurt, he still allowed me to tell others of him and see people give their hearts to him. He used me right where I was.

Was I always strong? No! But he was, and every time I grew weary or weak, he lent me *his* strength. When I did wrong or took a wrong turn, he turned me around and showed me how to get right. I may have had a mountain of pain and hurt and trials in my life that may have caused other to die, but I lived. He never once let go of me. He was there in the bad times, he was there in the good times, and he held me close to him at all times.

Because he gave me mercy, I can show mercy to others. Because he gave compassion, I can give compassion to others. Because he gave me *his* unconditional love, I can give unconditional love to others. His mercy is forever, and *his* love *is* forever. Reach out, for he is reaching out to you.

If this book touches but one life, it will be worth it all. There is no such a thing as a "throw away" person. For he loves us all and died for all! I am still learning, and I am still growing. If he brought me through all that he has in my lifetime, he can bring you through also.

With all my heart, I wish every reader the ability to understand the undying and unconditional love he has for each of you. He loves you because he created you. He didn't speak you into existence, but he, with *his* own hands, formed you individually. No one can be exactly like you. Just as everyone has their own DNA, so are you unique and one of a kind. There is only one of you. I pray with all of my heart that my life story and walk with the Lord would somehow touch you and awaken something inside of you to know him. I am a survivor! In him, through him, and with him, I have survived!

A HEART-TO-HEART MINISTRY

Thou, O God, didst send a plentiful rain, whereby thou didst confirm thine inheritance, when it was weary. Thy congregation hath dwelt therein: thou, O God, hast prepared of thy goodness for the poor. The Lord gave the word: great was the company of those that published it.

Psalm 68:9-11

*T*hese verses speak a lot to me because they symbolize where I was when I first started home to a church. I was drenched with the rain of trials and tribulations. I felt alone, hated, and had even tried suicide. But someone interceded for me, and I was never allowed to die. God had other plans for my life. But I didn't know that when I first came to the Lord and into a church.

I was rejected by my family, and the Lord had removed my husband from my home. My marriage had reached a point of no return. It was down to a choice: remain with Satan and all of his demons or be removed from all and dwell with God. I walked over into the river of life called

Jesus. I pray you will continue to follow for yourself the stepping stones of life that I followed.

The next step was *Psalm 61:2*, where it says, *"From the end of the earth will I cry unto thee, when my heart is overwhelmed: lead me to the rock that is higher than I."* As I prayed, the Lord told me to go to a certain church, where I had to go through an inner healing. This was the beginning of reliving many chapters in my life that I have attempted to share with you as we traveled together through my life.

I didn't know where this church was, but I did know who truly represented God and *his* love. So I started seeking out this church. When I found it, I received the counseling I needed and agreed to come to church on Sunday.

That first Sunday I came in obedience, but I have to be honest and say I was scared to death. Everything in me wanted to run out the back door. How can I talk to anyone of things I really did not want to remember? And yet if I did not get them out of inside me, they would eat me up alive.

You see, I never knew love or what love really was. And suddenly, I was in a room filled with people who talked, walked, and showed nothing but love. And here I was, afraid to love or to be loved. To me love was painful and hurtful, and I never wanted to be loved, but there was a hole in me that desperately wanted to be loved.

When the pastor started preaching, I heard God's love coming toward me. *Psalm 71:9-11* describes my feelings: *"Forsake me not when my strength faileth. For mine enemies speak against me; and they that lay wait for my soul take counsel together, saying, God hath forsaken him: persecute and take him; for there is none to deliver him."*

In my heart I had come to believe this. I didn't feel that anyone cared about me as a person. I was alone with my problems and didn't think anyone could possibly care enough to help me through. My family deserted me, my friends departed, and I was totally alone.

But here was this pastor, telling me God cared, and because *he* cared, she cared. I saw God's love come through her to me. As I listened that day, my soul was touched. My heart was totally given to God, and it is wholly *his* to do whatever he wants with it. My life is no longer what it was but is changed.

God gave me boldness to speak out for him and tell how he has changed my life. To show how fully it's changed would take a book. That is what this book is to be – a living testimony for my Lord, Jesus Christ, and what he can do. I asked God to give me a scripture to show what I felt when I first entered into a body of believing Christians and the feelings and changes that took place. He gave me *1 John 4:15-21:*

"Whosoever, shall confess that Jesus is the Son of God, God dwelleth in him, and he in God. And we have known and believed the love that God hath to us. God is love; and he that dwelleth in love dwelleth in God and God in him. Herein is our love made perfect, that we may have boldness in the Day of Judgment: because as he is, so are we in this world. There is no fear in love; but perfect love casteth out fear: because fear hath torment. He that feareth is not made perfect in love. We love him, because he first loved us. If a man says, I love God, and hateth his brother, he is a liar: for he that loveth not his brother whom he hath seen, how can he love God whom he hath not seen? And these commandments have we from him, that he who loveth God loves his brother also."

In *Isaiah 55:7,* it says, *"Let the wicked forsake his way, and the unrighteous man his thoughts: and let him return unto the Lord, and he will have mercy upon him, and to our God, for he will abundantly pardon."*

All I had to do was say, "Lord, forgive me. Take my life. It's yours," and he did. I praise and thank the good Lord for *his* love, compassion, and understanding. I thank all the godly people and ministers who planted seeds in my life along the way that taught me what true love is. For the first time in my life, I could honestly feel free to hug someone and say, "I love you," and then have someone else hug me and tell me they love me. It wasn't always so in my life.

God's grace is so good, and *his* love is so great that he's replaced my earthly family with a loving, caring, sharing Christian family that accepts me as I am with all my faults – that's Jesus! Pure and simply Jesus! The love and compassion of Jesus' heart flows freely to your heart. It's a ""heart-to-heart" ministry. That's what Jesus wants: heart-to-heart ministry done in unconditional love. Praise God. My heart was touched, and I was set free – not only to be loved, but to share *his* love with others.

The caterpillar has changed to a butterfly, and I'm going to tell everyone I can that Jesus is real. He *does* heal your hurts and sets you free to be the best you can possibly be.

All I can say is: "Thank you, Jesus! I'm free at last and home where I belong."

Today is a day of rejoicing. The flood waters came up, and I nearly drowned in the flood of trials and tribulations that beset me. I have weathered the surging floods of rejection, fires, incest, rape, cults, divorce (not once but three times), wife abuse, child abuse, sexual assaults on myself, condemnations, fears, loneliness, and ugly rumors grounded in lies and fed by gossipy mouths, and all of them trying to utterly destroy me both emotionally and physically.

These were the floods of my life – one wave after another would rise up and crash across the beach of my life.

With each wave, my life began to crumble and fall apart until there was only a shell of a person left. I was someone who had nothing more to give. Everything had been taken from me, including my self-respect.

But amidst all this, Jesus came down, and glory went up. I've been redeemed by the blood of the Lamb and am now living in *his* grace. Praise God! Every tear in that valley of tears was shed through trials and tribulations, and every one of them has turned into a story of *his* grace and mercy for me.

Genesis 912-15 says:

"And God said, this is the token of the covenant which I make between me and you and every living creature that is with you, for perpetual generations: I do set my bow in the cloud, and it shall be for a token of a covenant between me and the earth and it shall come to pass, when I bring a cloud over the earth, that the bow shall be seen in the cloud: and I will remember my covenant, which is between me and you and every living creature of all flesh, and the waters shall no more become a flood to destroy all flesh."

With these words, God brought me to my ability to love unconditionally *all* his creatures, all the hurting of the world. He gave me his caring heart and a deep understanding of *his* unconditional love.

SOME HELP FOR THE HURTING

I pray, as I have traveled backward and forward to Jesus with my life today that you will see that, no matter where you are, he brought me through the very same circumstances and emotions of perhaps where you *are* right now. And what he did for me, he will do for you.

Many have asked me what was it that kept me coming back to Jesus and what was it that kept me going. I was told a story in the Bible that I did not understand. Why God was always bringing me back to the same scripture in the Bible was soon to be evident as he revealed its meaning to me. But as time passed on, I went in and out of God's will for my life. I would approach *him* and then back off and repeat this cycle many times before a mature understanding of the word *he* had given to me was revealed in its fullness.

I want to share it with you now, and perhaps it will help you as much as it has helped me through the years and is still helping me to this day. It can be found in *Matthew 14:22-33*. I am going to break this verse down for you and explain it as it was shown to me many times when I thought I just could not go another day.

22) Immediately Jesus made the disciples get into the boat and go on ahead of him to the other side, while he dismissed the crowd.

23) After he had dismissed them, he went up on a mountainside by himself to pray. When evening came, he was there alone.

24) But the boat was already a considerable distance from land, buffered by the waves because the wind was against it.

Now I am going to explain what God showed me. Oftentimes Jesus is alone and away from us – at least it seems that is how we feel. So we do our own thing and wander throughout our days, doing things and facing our trials and circumstances alone and on our own terms. In verse 23, we find that Jesus went up on a mountainside to pray, and when evening came, he was alone, but he was still looking for those in the boat. And in verse 24, we find that he has spied them up ahead away from shore and the wind and waves beating against them.

You see, the boat is the safety zone – that place where we are most comfortable. You might even call it your comfort zone. You feel safe as you are in your comfort zone and comfortable in the circumstances you are in. Yet you don't like the circumstances, so fear besets you as the winds and waves try to overtake and capsize your boat of comfort. You feel alone and frightened, not realizing that *he is* looking for you and has already spotted you and is watching over you.

> *During the fourth watch of the night Jesus went out to them, walking on the lake.*

> *Matthew 14:25 (NIV)*

Jesus was already waiting on top of *all* their (your) circumstances and trials. He conquered them *all* at the cross. His shed blood covered whatever circumstance or trial you have or are going through. But notice *he is* coming toward his disciples, *not* away from them. Jesus is always walking toward you. The word says that *he* will never leave you or forsake you. How comforting that was to know

> *When the disciples saw him walking on the lake, they were terrified. It's a ghost, they said, and cried out in fear.*

> *Matthew 14:26 INIV)*

Why would they call out in fear? Why would you or I cry out in fear? Somewhere deep inside each of us is the thought process that because we have done wrong or are not good enough for Jesus, we tend to fear him and become afraid when we come face-to-face with *him*. It is like a little child who had been stealing cookies out of the cookie jar and one day gets caught with his hand in the jar as he looks up and sees his mom or dad standing there looking at him. Fear instantly takes a hold of the child. So it was with the disciples. They saw the Lord coming toward them and were fearful. Up until that moment, no one had ever walked on water, and naturally, they thought they were seeing things and became afraid. Afraid of this unknown apparition walking toward them – was it reality or imagined? What mixed feeling those disciples must have had at that moment. But not one of them could deny that *he* was on top of the water walking toward them.

Jesus took care of our circumstances when he died on the cross. *He* is indeed on top of our circumstances and trials. And *he* wants us to be also. So even in the midst of the storms of our lives, *he* is present and *he* is coming toward us, not away from us.

> *But Jesus immediately said to them: take courage. It is I. Don't be afraid.*
>
> *Matthew 14:27 (NIV)*

Is that not what *he* is still saying to us today? Take courage; I am here; don't be afraid. I will walk through this with you. How comforting it was to me to know that *he* came to me and helped me through each trial and each circumstance that life threw at me. I could not do it in self, and I did not have the courage in self to conquer anything in my life. But with *him* at my side, and as I drew on *his* comfort and strength, I had the courage to stand strong and go on and deal with all my circumstances and trials and, yes, errors on my part. I made bad judgments based on what I knew in my own life experiences, but with *his* help in showing me these things and helping me overcome them all, I did conqueror and go on.

> *"Lord if it's you," Peter replied. "Tell me to come to you on the water."*
>
> *Matthew 14:28 (NIV)*

Is that not what we all do? We are all so full of insecurities and doubts. Peter had doubts it was Jesus before him. Did not Peter say, "If it is you?" Now that is doubt, for sure. I know I was doubtful that Jesus or anyone could ever stop the merry-go-round of bad things in my life, yet I was reaching out to *him* and all the time *he* was reaching out to me. But I had to go through all these things in my life to understand the grace and mercy of *his* heart. *He* was the whole time stretching my faith muscles and giving me understanding and placing things in my life and heart of hearts.

> *"Come," he said. Then Peter got down out of the boat walked on the water, and came towards Jesus.*
>
> *Matthew 14:29 (NIV)*

Peter gathered faith that it was indeed Jesus who had sought him out and that he could go to Jesus, no matter what. He stepped out of the boat (his safety and comfort zone) and walked into the storm (his circumstances and trials) head-on, keeping his eyes on Jesus the whole time. And because his eyes were on Jesus and not on the storm (circumstances, and trials or even the boat – his safety and comfort zone), he too walked on top of the water (everything that was coming against him in life).

> *But when he saw the wind, he was afraid and beginning to sink, cried out, "Lord save me!"*

> *Matthew 14:30 (NIV)*

Peter was keeping his eyes on Jesus, and then all of a sudden, he was sinking back into the storm with its waters and winds. His circumstances once again beset him. Oh, how many times did I take my eyes off of Jesus and begin to sink in my problems, circumstances, and trials? But when I cried out to Jesus – he was there to reach down and pull me out. Each time *he* was faithful to bring me out of it all. And something wonderful happens when we cry, "Lord, save me." Jesus stops what *he* is doing and *he* comes to our side and pulls us out time and time again. You can see that, like Peter, when I took my eyes off of Jesus, I too sank back into circumstances I did not really want in my life.

Immediately Jesus reached out HIS hand and caught him. "You of little faith," he said. "Why did you doubt?"

Matthew 14:31 (NIV)

When Peter took his eyes off Jesus, he sank, and doubt crept in. That is what happens to each of us. Doubt creeps in, and the enemy starts whispering in our ears, "Boy, you have done it now. No one, not even Jesus, will want to be around you now." Or maybe, "There is no turning back now. Might as well keep on being and doing what you are doing because no one really cares and you are all alone now." Well, we need to flex our faith muscles and tell the old devil and the voices telling these us things that we are indeed worthy. You see, we are worthy not in ourselves but only through the shed blood of Jesus. We can't have faith unless we have something to believe in. Thank God; *he* truly does care. And *his* blood washes us *all* clean and makes us acceptable.

Our sins are washed in the blood and thrown into the sea of forgetfulness, never to be remembered. The only time any of the memories of the past are allowed to creep back up into my memory bank is to help another come through the things that I have done. My experiences and circumstances are teaching lessons for others. Because what *he* did for me, *he* will do for you.

And when they climbed into the boat the wind died down.

Matthew 14:32 (NIV)

You notice that Jesus and Peter climbed into the boat together. Mind you, the boat was their safety zone and comfort zone. They were used to the circumstances and trials. However, this time, they entered the boat together, Peter was no longer alone to face the storms of life. Jesus was with him there. And *he* was with the others also. Just as *he* is with me, he wants to be with you. All we have to do is ask *him* and let *him* enter into the storms of life. Together we will face all the storms, circumstances, and trials that life has to offer us.

And then those that were in the boat worshipped him, saying, "Truly you are the son of God."

Matthew 14:33 (NIV)

I may have been riding along life in my own boat, but there were others in the same boat. And once Peter brought the Lord into his boat, he was able to show the others in the same boat his Lord and Savior. And they realized that what Jesus had just done for Peter, *he* would do for them. And they all praised the Lord. The disciples acknowledged *him* as the Son of God. So I say to each and every one of you that what *he* has done for me *he* will do for you.

The story of Peter walking on top of the water with Jesus has helped me through years of much turmoil. Yes, my life has not been an easy life, but I will say this much: *if* I had not gone through these things in life, I would not have the heart of compassion and love for others that I do today. I would not understand that the heart of God is one of love for all *his* creation. And we are all *his* creation. *He* truly care about each of us.

Will you give Jesus a place in your life and heart so he can come into your boat (life) and give you his comfort and peace? *He* will help you walk through the circumstances and trials and the sudden storms of life. If no one cares at all and you feel alone, know that Jesus cares and so do I. Jesus is there right now at your side, waiting for you to reach out your hand. He will take your hand and pull you out of those storms of life, whatever they may be. *He* will not only pull you out but put you on the path you need to walk on and give you joy.

> *If thou shalt confess with thy mouth the Lord Jesus and shalt believe in thine heart that God hath raised him from the dead, thou shalt be saved. For with the heart man believeth unto righteousness; and with the mouth confession is made unto salvation. For the scripture saith; whosoever believeth on him shall not be ashamed.* Romans 10:9-11

Will you take Jesus as your Lord and Savior? If so, pray this prayer. Lord Jesus, I am a sinner, and I recognize I need you. I believe you died for my sins, and only through faith in you and through your death and resurrection can I be forgiven. I turn from my sins and ask you to come into my heart and life as my Lord and Savior. From this day forth, I will, with your help, live my life in a way that's pleasing to you. I thank you, Lord Jesus, for coming into my life and heart and saving me. In Jesus' name I pray. Amen

Congratulations, you are now a child of God. Go and tell someone.

This is my prayer for you: Father, in Jesus' name I bring before you this child/person reading this book, as well as all the victims of those types of abuse. I place each one on your throne. Lord, I ask that you comfort their hearts and give them your peace. I ask that the healing process begin in their lives. I pray that you will cause your holy boldness to rise up in their spirit to reach out and get that necessary help that they need right now. Send the mighty warring angels to them to deliver, protect, and come to their side as they reach out to get help. I also ask you to hide them in the cleft of your wings and surround them with your love and tender mercies. Lord, cause a stirring in the hearts of the neighbors, school authorities, police and churches to open their eyes and do what is right; let them not rest until they have sought help on behalf of those who are hurting. Give these people a boldness to do what is right. Let no man turn a blind eye anymore. Bring awareness to each individual when these things are happening around them so they may reach out their hand and bring these victims to safety until the authorities can get to them. In Jesus' name I pray. Amen and amen.

If you are in immediate danger now, please call 911 to get help. I have also asked permission to give these hotline numbers, as well as their websites, so that you can talk to someone who cares and can point you in the right direction to get the help you need.

> National Domestic Violence Hotline and website
> http://www.thehotline.org/get-help/
> 1-800-799-7233
> Rape, Abuse, Incest National Network
> http://www.rainn.org
> 1-800-656-4673

If anyone feels alone and unloved and just needs an ear to listen or a shoulder to lean on, feel free to contact me via email at mousielady@comcast.net, and in the subject line, place the words *message for Grace* and I will answer you. Know that Jesus cares and loves you, and so do I. You are not alone. And what *he* has done for me – *he* will do for you!

May my life story touch you in a positive way and be an encouragement to you. I want you to know that, no matter what, he *will* be there for you and bring you through and that one day you too shall touch lives. God bless you!

I write this account of my life *not* to glorify the working of the devil and the circumstances I survived but to glorify the Lord of lords and King of kings who delivered me out of the lion's den and kept me from being eaten alive and utterly destroyed. He set me free to glorify the God of deliverance. He whom the Lord has set free is free indeed.

DEDICATION

This book is dedicated to the Lord and his undying love for all the hurting of the world. To those who don't realize their self-worth, you are unique. It's about time that you start viewing yourself as you really are – a special gift from God!

> *Before I formed you in the womb, I knew you, before you were born, I set you apart...*
> *Jeremiah 1:5*

> *When I was woven together in the depts. Of the earth, your eyes saw my unformed body. All the days ordained for me were written in your book before one of them came to be.*
> *Psalm 139:15b-16*

God is perfect. He is the great I AM. Everything he has made is a miracle, and everything he continues to show and give us is a blessing. Would the God who created the heavens and the earth do a half-hearted job? The answer is no. So look at yourself today. Do you realize that God created every special part of you? You are one of God's masterpieces. He made you in his image. He made you special. He made you beautiful. That's right – he made you his very own beautiful creation. He has given you creative and special gifts that are not like anyone else's. He has given you a unique personality and temperament. He has created every little special detail of you and your life.

So take pride in yourself. Not the kind of pride that goes before God, but a pride that says, "I am unique and special to God." Do not allow the media and all the negative reports make you take your eyes off all the positives that God has given to you. Develop your talents and use them for God's lorry. Polish your good looks. Fatten up the fruits that the Holy Spirit has given to you and then display them proudly for his glory. Accept yourself for who you are – a child of God. Oh, how blessed we are to be able to say that. Repeat it, "I am a child of God, and I am special." So don't worry about what others think about you. Let the God who created you show you the beauty inside of you. That means that you must look for your value in him alone. Be encouraged, because you are so special to God.

Marilyn Leck

Grace Under Fire